LONDON'S TRANSPORT

From Roman Times to the Present Day

LONDON'S TRANSPORT

From Roman Times to the Present Day

Anthony Burton

PEN & SWORD
TRANSPORT

AN IMPRINT OF PEN & SWORD BOOKS LTD.
YORKSHIRE – PHILADELPHIA

First published in Great Britain in 2022 by
Pen and Sword Transport
An imprint of
Pen & Sword Books Ltd.
Yorkshire - Philadelphia

Copyright © Anthony Burton, 2022

ISBN 978 1 39908 586 1

The right of Anthony Burton to be identified as author of this work has been asserted by him in accordance with the Copyright, Designs and Patents Act 1988.

A CIP catalogue record for this book is available from the British Library.

All rights reserved. No part of this book may be reproduced or transmitted in any form or by any means, electronic or mechanical including photocopying, recording or by any information storage and retrieval system, without permission from the Publisher in writing.

Typeset in 10.5/13.5 pt Palatino by SJmagic DESIGN SERVICES, India.

Printed and bound in India by Replika Press Pvt. Ltd.

Pen & Sword Books Ltd incorporates the imprints of Pen & Sword Books Archaeology, Atlas, Aviation, Battleground, Discovery, Family History, History, Maritime, Military, Naval, Politics, Railways, Select, Transport, True Crime, Fiction, Frontline Books, Leo Cooper, Praetorian Press, Seaforth Publishing, Wharncliffe and White Owl.

For a complete list of Pen & Sword titles please contact

PEN & SWORD BOOKS LIMITED
47 Church Street, Barnsley, South Yorkshire, S70 2AS, England
E-mail: enquiries@pen-and-sword.co.uk
Website: www.pen-and-sword.co.uk

or

PEN AND SWORD BOOKS
1950 Lawrence Rd, Havertown, PA 19083, USA
E-mail: Uspen-and-sword@casematepublishers.com
Website: www.penandswordbooks.com

Contents

	Introduction	6
Chapter One	The Beginnings	7
Chapter Two	Roads, Carriages and Omnibuses	20
Chapter Three	Crossing the Thames	48
Chapter Four	The Railway Age	70
Chapter Five	Train Travel in the Steam Age	98
Chapter Six	The Underground	113
Chapter Seven	Trams and Trolleys	128
Chapter Eight	Motor Vehicles	138
Chapter Nine	Aviation	155
Chapter Ten	Recent Developments	166
	Further Reading	176
	Acknowledgements	177
	Index	178

Introduction

I dealt with water transport in London in an earlier volume – *Maritime London* – so this book will be looking at road, rail and air transport in London from the earliest times to the present day. Defining London chronologically is simple: it begins with the establishment of Londinium in the first century CE. Defining it geographically is rather more complex. For centuries, London was defined as the walled city – so that, for example, Westminster was then a separate place altogether. Then, over the centuries, the city grew, swallowing up what had once been quite distinct villages, such as Hampstead, and in more recent times it has also eaten up large parts of the old counties of Essex and Middlesex. I have taken a rather pragmatic approach, basing the story largely on what we would now regard as central London, but allowing excursions further out into the suburbs as the story changes with the years.

There is another problem that always comes up with writing history, especially when it involves technology: which units do you use – the ones in use at the time or the ones we officially use today? I have gone with the historical method, simply because they make sense in the context. If an engineer in the nineteenth century specified that he wanted a steam cylinder to be 24 inch diameter, he would not have asked the manufacturer to provide one at 60.96 cm. But, of course, when we come to the modern era, decimalization has changed everything, so I shall be using the units of today. The last problem is money. Again, decimalization has introduced new units, but younger readers might like to know that before that we had 20 shillings in a pound, and 12 pennies in a shilling. Values have, of course, changed dramatically, even in a few decades. Even a modern penny coin is generally regarded as much a nuisance as a valuable item to be cherished. For example, that old penny two centuries ago had roughly the purchasing power of one pound today.

CHAPTER ONE

The Beginnings

The story has a natural starting point: the foundation of Londinium, the Roman name for London, in the first century CE. This was a comparatively small settlement and had hardly had time to get organized before it was totally demolished. The trouble started with the death of the Iceni king Prasutagus, at which point the Roman rulers declared that it was their right to now claim not only his property but also that of all the nobles of his court. His widow, Boudica, was not surprisingly outraged and objected to the grabbing of all these possessions. The Roman response was to have her flogged and her daughters raped. This was sufficient for Boudica to arouse the Iceni to follow her in a war against the Romans. After initial successes, the Iceni marched on Londinium, which was then abandoned. Boudica's success was short lived and once the rebellion had been quelled, Londinium was rebuilt, this time within solid stone walls. Excavation has revealed the extent of this new city. The walls spread along the north bank of the Thames from the present sites of the Tower of London to just short of Blackfriars railway bridge: the northern edge is still remembered in the name of the street, London Wall. At about the same time, the Romans also constructed the first bridge across the river.

Londinium was now, in effect, the capital of Roman Britain, and although it has long since been built over many times, we know that its streets would have been laid out in a regular grid, in the same way as other towns had been throughout the Roman empire. The Romans were not in the habit of changing their ways just because they had arrived in a different country, so the best way of imagining how a Londinium street might have looked is to turn to the site where devastation caused a great tragedy yet preserved an amazing amount of physical remains: Pompeii. Here, we can see streets paved with large flat stones, with deep ruts cut over the years by the passage of heavily laden carts. On either side are the pavements, with substantial kerbs, mainly around 30 cm high. There are stepping stones for pedestrians to cross the roads – a lot of them, far more than in other Roman cities. Why were they needed?

One has to remember that all the traffic of the town was pulled by animals who, to put it delicately, were not exactly toilet trained: the stones kept Roman feet clear of the muck.

The capital was also the hub from which major roads led out to the other main Roman centres. We have given them names, such as Akeman Street and Watling Street, but we have no record of what the Romans themselves called them. Using modern place names, the main road heading south went to Canterbury, where it split off into branches to four ports – Richborough, Dover, Lympne and Reculver. There was another route to the Channel port of Chichester. Heading westward, the road led to Silchester, and again divided with branches to Portchester, Exeter and Caerleon. Two routes led north: one to Chester that was then continued on to Carlisle; and the other to York, again continued on to Hadrian's Wall and Corbridge. Finally, the eastern route led to Colchester. The one thing everyone thinks they know about Roman roads is that they are straight. This is not strictly true. The Roman military engineers who were responsible for surveying and building the routes took the most direct route that was possible, but they always had to take the landscape into account. Some years ago, I walked following the route of Akeman Street from Cirencester and where it reached the valley of the River Reach, the line of the ancient road

The Via di Nola street in Pompeii, showing the high kerbs and stepping stones for pedestrians to cross clear of the mud. London streets would presumably have looked similar.

was clear, running in a sweeping curve to make an easier gradient. What they did not have to worry about was getting permission from local landowners; their views were immaterial as far as the Romans were concerned.

This great network must have made Londinium itself into an extremely busy place. There would have been essential supplies coming in from overseas, which for anyone of Italian origins would certainly have included wine and olive oil. There would be produce arriving from the surrounding countryside to feed the population, and as this was the capital there were edicts and instructions to be sent to the legions based all over the country. All this depended on roads that were suitable to take such a heavy traffic. In Britain, the main roads were generally built up above the surrounding ground on the 'agger', rather like a causeway, with drainage ditches to the side. The final surface of large flat stones was laid on solid foundations. There were milestones along the way set at Roman mile intervals – roughly 1,480 metres. These were cylindrical stone pillars, generally about two metres high. There were post stations along the way at anything from 6 to 16 Roman miles, where horses

A well-preserved section of Roman road in Syria. It shows the characteristic raised agger and large stone slabs. It can also be seen to have a pronounced curve.

could be changed and with rest houses for travellers, slightly further apart. This was a very efficient posting system, the *cursus publicus*, and was only available to official couriers who either travelled on horseback or in vehicles.

Londinium traffic would have had a great variety; local carts and wagons, chariots, the couriers coming and going, taking edicts out into the country at large and returning with news of life in the rest of Britain. Carts bringing in produce from the farms would often have solid plank wheels, but those used for longer journeys had spoked wheels. The latter could be two-wheeled vehicles for fast journeys or four-wheeled and covered with a cloth or leather awning for longer journeys and for baggage trains. They seem to have been comparatively crude, with fixed axles. Horses were shod, so the streets would have been alive with the metallic clatter of hooves. But by the beginning of the fifth century, Roman rule in Britain came to an end and with it Londinium's importance began to shrink. In Anglo-Saxon Britain, there was no longer a single country, controlled from the capital, but a whole series of independent kingdoms. Roman streets and roads deteriorated, partly through neglect and partly because they were a handy source of building stone. We know very little about traffic in those years and even less about life in the decaying city of London. The capital, however, was to regain its former importance following the Norman invasion of 1066.

In theory, all roads linking towns were King's Highways, and it was the duty of local landowners to keep them in a good state of repair. It was a system that clearly failed, for as late as the eighteenth century, commentators were complaining about the way in which it was implemented. John Hawkins described it in his *Observations on the State of the Highway* of 1763.

A roman milestone from the western end of Hadrian's Wall, preserved in the Tullie House Museum, Carlisle.

Let us now see in what Manner the Law at present under Consideration is observed in those few Parishes, where the Inhabitants are

A drawing by Alan Sorrell of an entrance to Londinium, with a typical cart of the period.

disposed to yield obedience to the Letter of it: the Days for performing the Statute Duty are so far from being considered as Days of Labour, that as well as the Farmers as the common Day-Labourers, have long been used to look on them as Holidays, as a kind of Recess from their accustomed Labour, and devoted to Idleness and its concomitant Indulgencies of Riot and Drunkenness.

The surveyor of roads, who was supposed to oversee the operation, was allowed to abandon any attempt to get the locals to do the work and try to raise money from them instead to pay labourers. Unfortunately, according to Hawkins, the results were no better as the surveyor rarely understood road building and the workforce had no experience. It was, he wrote, 'a Contest between Ignorance armed with Authority on the one side, and invincible Obstinacy on the other.'

It might seem that this had little to do with London, but the city was entirely dependent on the roads to provide the essentials of life. The outlying farms, for example, would provide the basic food for the community. Livestock could be driven into the city for slaughter, but grain had to be taken in carts to the mill for grinding into flour and then distributed around the city. We know there was a water mill at Bromley-on-Bow in the eleventh century because it was recorded in the Domesday Book. A sixteenth century map of London shows the area outside the city walls as being open countryside, with two windmills, just north of the present site of Moorgate underground station. There are still mill buildings at Bromley, though no longer grinding grain, and a windmill has been preserved at Brixton. These are survivors of many more that would have been needed to keep the growing population of London fed – it all helped to add to a constant stream of traffic, carts and packhorses on the roads leading into and out of the city. The fourteenth century Gough Map shows a web of cart routes, centred on London. Thomas Dekker, writing in 1609 in *The Seven Deadly Sins of London*, presents the streets as a cacophony.

> In every street, carts and Coaches make such a thundering as if the world ranne upon wheeles; at everie corner, men, women and children meete in such shoales, that postes are sette up of purpose to strengthen the houses, least with such jostling one another they should shoulder them downe. Besides, hammers are beating in one place. Tubs, hooping in another, Pots clinking in a third, water-tankards running at tilt in a fourth: here are Porters, sweating under burdens, Chapmen (as if they were at Leape frog) skippe out of one shop into another: Tradesmen (as if they were dancing Galliards) are as lusty at legges and never stand still: all are as busie as countrie Attorneys at an Assizes.

Brixton windmill is one of the many windmills that once existed in the London area. When it was built, it was still surrounded by open fields.

The city streets themselves were maintained by a variety of different means. Pavage was a toll applied to traffic that was used to pay for making and maintaining the streets. Sometimes wealthy individuals made grants for road improvement and more than thirty roads in and around London were paved in this way in the fourteenth and fifteenth centuries. Royalty occasionally got involved, and in the fourteenth century, Edward III ordered the road linking the City to Westminster to be paved. By this date, street maintenance had become more organized in London. In 1280, London aldermen were required to appoint four 'respectable' men to clean and repair the streets. A century later, the two tasks had been divided between 'scawageours' – later known as scavengers – who were responsible for keeping the streets clean, and paviers who were responsible for construction and repair. The work of the former was overseen by the surveyor of streets and of the latter by the stone master. The scavengers were not the only ones who were supposed to do their bit to keep the streets reasonably clean. Citizens were supposed to be responsible for keeping the areas in front of their houses cleaned once a week and were required either to take the rubbish to one of the dung heaps outside the city walls or dump it in the river. The little River Fleet was to become notorious for the filth that polluted its waters.

Originally, anyone could be recruited into the work of paving, whether they had experience or not. But over time, paving became a recognized craft, and the paviers had their own guild by 1479. They received regular wages, which were fixed using rules that had been laid out in an ordnance of 1301. They provided different surfaces for different parts of the city. For the important streets they would use cobbles and sand but for the side lanes they would use gravel. Potholes were simply filled in with twigs and stone chippings, and when a street needed repaving, the old surface was seldom removed. A new level was simply added on top, so that street levels kept rising. No machinery was available, so the streets were simply compacted by hand. There do not appear to be any illustrations of medieval London paviers at work, but a fifteenth century German work shows a pavier sitting on a one-legged stool, ramming home cobbles (left).

A fifteenth century illustration of a pavier setting in cobbles, while sitting on a one-legged stool.

One might have expected that with this degree of control, all would be well, but a Venetian visitor, Andreas Franciscius, wrote of his visit in 1489:

> All the streets are so badly paved that they get wet at the slightest quantity of water, and this happens very frequently owing to the large numbers of cattle carrying water, as well as on account of the rain, of which there is a great deal in this island. Then

a vast amount of evil-smelling mud is formed, which does not disappear quickly but lasts a long time, in fact nearly the whole year round.

There was one other important part to the road system of London: the crossing of the Thames. The old Roman bridge fell into disrepair, and as the river formed a boundary between what were now two hostile states, there was no rush to replace it. The date of the next bridge is uncertain but took place at some time near the end of the tenth century under Saxon rule, only to be destroyed again a few years later. The bridges seemed fated to be short lived for a time. A new bridge was completed immediately following the Norman conquest of 1066, only to be destroyed in a fierce storm in 1091. Replaced in the reign of William II, the next catastrophe was destruction by fire. Once again it had to be rebuilt and the last of the timber bridges was completed in 1163. The construction of the first stone bridge was an act of penance by Henry II, following the murder of Thomas Becket, the Archbishop of Canterbury, in 1170. The work began six years after his death but was only finished in 1209 and a prominent feature was the chapel in the centre, devoted to Thomas Becket, who had been canonized. It became the official starting point for the pilgrimage to Canterbury, made famous by Geoffrey Chaucer. The bridge was constructed on nineteen arches, with a drawbridge in the centre, which would allow small vessels with masts to pass through.

Today, we think of bridges as no more than a means of getting over an obstacle, but the old London bridge was a street like any other, lined with shops. One can see something similar today in Pulteney Bridge in Bath. There were gatehouses at either end. Throughout the years, the number of shops and houses on the bridge kept increasing, until by Tudor times there may have been as many as 200 huddled together. There were also two latrines on the bridge, which discharged straight into the river underneath, which must have been a novel sort of hazard for boatmen. The bridge not only crossed the river but divided it. It formed a barrier to large seagoing vessels, which were confined to the Pool of London, downstream. Smaller vessels plied the waters above the bridge. Although, in theory, it provided a valuable crossing for Londoners, in practice, it was a bottleneck, simply too narrow to take heavy traffic. As a result, the river became the main means of getting from

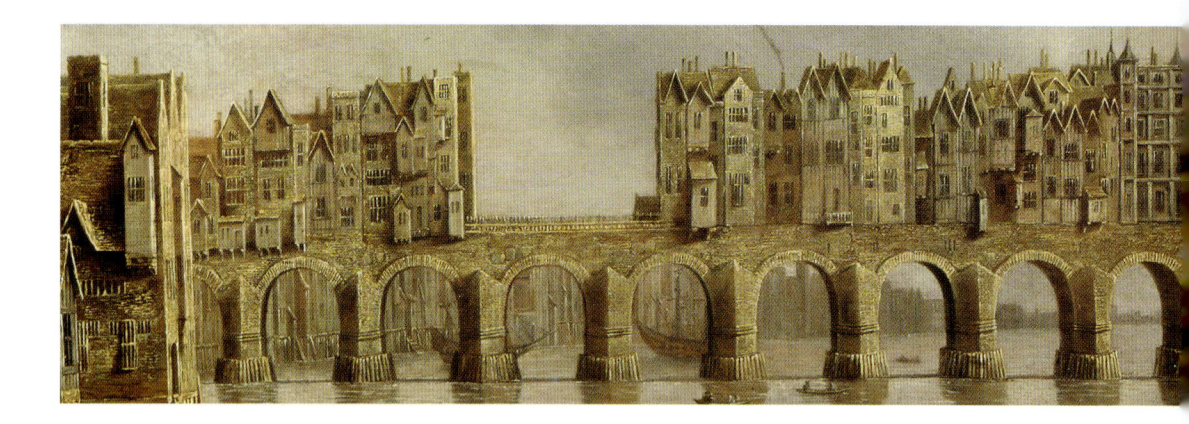

The old London Bridge, with its rows of shops and chapel in the centre, painted by the Dutch artist Claude de Jongh in the seventeenth century.

one side to the other as well as for travelling up stream and down. It was to remain in use for centuries, only replaced in 1831.

We do not know a great deal about the vehicles using the streets of London in medieval times, but as the quote above indicates, oxen were used for carriage as well as horses. Throughout the period, there were problems with cart wheels damaging the road surface. There were attempts to control this by a variety of means. One was to specify which of the city gates could be used for any particular type of traffic. Laws were passed, specifying that wheels had to be broad, the width depending on the size of the vehicle. Iron tyres were sometimes banned, but carters got round that by using metal studs in the wheel rim, which caused even worse damage. An alternative was to allow the spokes to extend right through the felloes, so that they also acted as studs to prevent wear on the

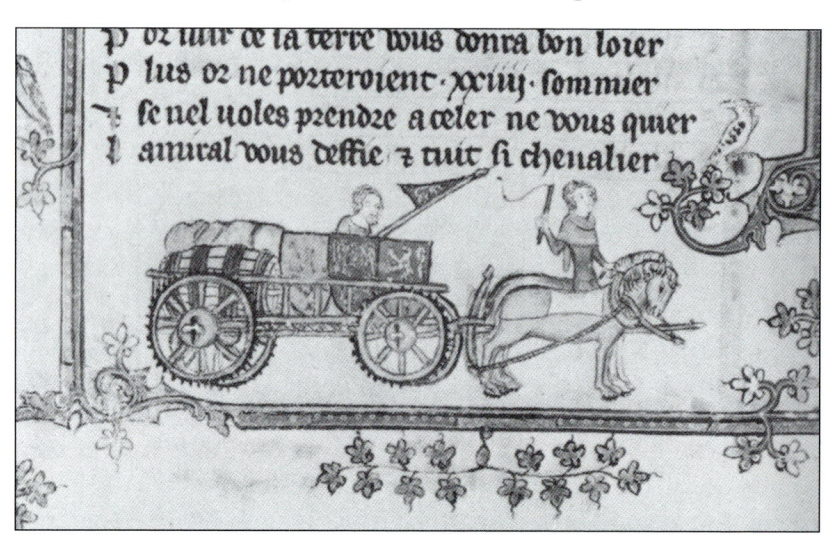

A farm cart with studded wheels from a fourteenth century Flemish manuscript.

wheel itself. By the later Middle Ages, the wheel had become far more sophisticated, with dished rims, which spread the load as the wagon swayed from side to side.

The craft of the wheelwright has scarcely changed since those days, so that when I went to visit Mike Rowland and Son, wheelwrights and coach builders in Devon, I was able to get a glimpse of centuries' old craftsmanship. There are four main components of the wheel: the hub; the spokes; the rim; and the tyre. The hub is traditionally made of elm, which is a very close-grained wood. The hub is marked out, sawn into rough shape and then turned on a lathe. In Devon, the lathe is a modern power tool, but the most common lathe in the earlier period was the pole lathe. The lathe had a treadle, with a cord attached, that was wrapped round the piece of wood to be turned. The other end of the cord was fastened to the pole made of a springy wood. The lathe turns as the treadle is pressed down, and the turner applies the chisel, and the cord pulls the pole down. Then the treadle is released, and the spring of the pole carries it back up to the starting position. Much of the work was often done in woodland – a major wheelwright industry grew up in the Chiltern Hills. The spokes are roughly shaped and finished off – and again the technique remains unchanged. The wheelwright sits on a bench known as a spoke horse, again equipped with a treadle, and uses a tool with double handles to shape the spoke – a tool still called a spokeshave. The rim is constructed of segments, known as felloes. The wheelwright would have a whole set of templates he could use to get the correct shape. The spokes were first fitted into the hub using mortise and tenon joints. After that, the felloes were added to complete the wheel. If an iron tyre was to be added, the joints all had to be slightly loose. The iron tyre was put on a fire and when it was red hot placed over the wheel, then rapidly cooled by dowsing in water. The tyre shrinks as it cools, drawing all the elements of the wheel into a perfect fit. Adding the tyre is very dramatic, accompanied by flames and clouds of steam and smoke. The changes affected every aspect of travel ion and around the capital, from improvement in road construction to major changes in the way in which vehicles were constructed and services were delivered.

One area that did show improvement from Roman times was the harness used for draught animals. By the twelfth century, illustrations show horses and oxen fitted with padded collars that look very like the modern horse collar in use today. However, very little had been done to improve matters for travellers. Coaches were rare, and were little better than covered carts, stuffed with cushions. The wealthy travelled on horseback but ladies who were unable or unwilling to ride were provided with whirlicotes. These were basically just wagon frames with hammocks slung between

An illustration from Diderot's *Encyclopédie* of 1769, showing wheelwrights at work. The men on the right are fitting a hot metal tyre onto the wheel with clouds of smoke and steam.

A broad-wheeled covered wagon, one of a series of drawings by W.H. Pyne of all kinds of eighteenth-century road vehicles.

them. Given the state of the roads and streets, travelling in one of these swaying devices must have been about as comfortable and nauseating as being caught in a storm at sea in an open boat. The majority of Londoners simply walked. Real changes in transport only really began to get under way in the seventeenth century.

CHAPTER TWO

Roads, Carriages and Omnibuses

Road improvement began to develop in the seventeenth century with the spread of turnpike roads, which were established by parliament, privately financed and the costs recouped by charging tolls. The first to be treated in this way was part of the Great North Road, which linked London to Scotland, starting at Smithfield Market. Most of the turnpikes, however, were built somewhat later in the eighteenth century, many in and around London. There was a spurt of activity in the 1720s, when 71 turnpike Acts were passed, and the numbers just kept on growing, until by 1830, Britain had a staggering 3,783 turnpike trusts. The authorizing Act would set out just what the Turnpike Trustees could charge, usually in great detail to ensure that no type of vehicle was missed out and could pass without payment. For example, horse drawn vehicles were charged different amounts, depending on the number of horses employed. In a typical Act, a coach pulled by six horses was charged four shillings but one with just a single horse was only charged a shilling. The authorities were still favouring broad-wheeled vehicles, so that a cart with wheels more than six inches wide paid four shillings, but ones with narrower wheels had to cough up an extra sixpence. So it went on for different categories, varying from a charge of just two pence for a man on a horse to ten pence per twenty for a flock of sheep being driven on the road. On some roads, the toll collector had his own house from which he collected the money. In others, there was simply a gate to be manned. Distances did not have to be very great to incur a fee. Londoners heading across Hampstead Heath, for example, would have had to stop at the toll house opposite the Spaniards Inn.

On the whole, the system worked in improving the roads, but there were inevitable problems. John Scott, in his *Digests of the General Highway and Turnpike Laws* of 1778, maintained that the problem lay with 'farming' out the tolls: handing over responsibility of maintenance to the highest bidder.

> The Trustees, when once a road is *farmed*, have nothing to do, but meet once a year to eat Venison, and pay the *Farmer*

his Annuity: the *Farmer* has nothing to do, but to do as little work, and pocket as much Money as he possibly can; he has other *Fish to fry*, other Matters to mend, than *Road-mending*: Incroachment after Incroachment takes place, the Hedge and the Trees grow till they meet overhead, the Landholders are excused from their Statute-duty, and the Water and the narrow-wheeled Waggons complete the Business. At length, perhaps, the universal Complaint of Travellers, or Menaces of Indictment, rouse the Trustees for Moment, a Meeting is called, the *Farmer* sent for and reprimanded, and a few Loads of Gravel buried among the Mud, serve to keep the Way barely passable.

The Norwich and London stage passing through a toll gate. The little toll house stands next to the gate, and the toll collector is being thrown the appropriate money.

Whatever the shortcomings of the system, there is little doubt that the turnpikes represented an improvement on what had gone before. But it was not until the end of the eighteenth century that there were any real developments in the way that roads were actually built. There was still some way to go, however, before the British caught up with what had been happening across the Channel in France. In 1716, during the reign of Louis XV, the government set up an official Corps des Ponts et Chaussés – bridges and roads corps – together with a school for training civil engineers. Pierre Trésaguet developed a new way of making roads in the 1770s. He had a first layer of stones placed on edge, not laid flat, then beaten down with a hammer. Above that was a second bed of stones, roughly broken, so that they could fill in any gaps in the foundation. The final layer was to be of the hardest available stones, each reduced to the size of a walnut, and arranged to form a curved surface to ensure good drainage. It was to be some years before such systems were introduced into Britain, notably by Thomas Telford. His system also had a layer of stones on edge as a foundation, followed by smaller stones arranged to a depth of 7 inches at the crown of the road and sloping down to three inches at the sides. The centre was then covered with small stones, stamped down by horses and the whole road completed by a thick layer of gravel. Telford used this system in his work on the Holyhead Road, an essential link for the mails from London to Ireland. Telford was keen to stress the importance of road making being 'considered as a separate and very important business … Hitherto road-making and repairing have not had sufficient importance attached to them.' His work earned him a punning title coined by his friend, the poet Robert Southey: 'The Colossus of Roads'.

Telford unquestionably built good roads, but at great expense. It was another engineer, John Loudon McAdam, who devised a way of creating roads that were as good as Telford's but far

Road building in the turnpike age: another of W.H. Pyne's illustrations.

cheaper to build. He realized that good, dry soil was itself a sufficiently good foundation as long as it could be kept dry. This was managed by using carefully graded stones, hammered down to create a compact surface. McAdam reported that in the years up to 1814 he had travelled some 30,000 miles inspecting and advising on roads, and all without any payment: 'my sole object having been to promote and extend a better and more economical system of road management, in the pursuit of which, success has exceeded my most sanguine expectations.' Not only did he travel at his own expense, but he also made a point of visiting sites at the worst time of year to make sure he saw the most damaging conditions that he would have to deal with. The results were, indeed, excellent, as the surveyor and superintendent of mail coaches recorded when giving evidence to a Parliamentary Select Committee. 'Wherever I have found anything done by Mr. McAdam's immediate direction, or by his pupils, or even in imitation of his principles, the improvement has been most decisive, and the superiority over the common method of repairing roads most evident.' His system is not to be confused with tarmacadam, which was only introduced in 1902. It was stated that by 1814, when the Committee sat, Britain had 19,725 miles of turnpikes, but 95,104 miles of other unimproved roads. There was still a lot to be done, but at least it meant that people could now expect to travel in reasonable comfort between the main towns and cities. It was thanks to the road improvements that manufacturers were able to start constructing new improved coaches and carriages. Before that, very few would have contemplated a journey in an unsprung vehicle on a rutted, bumpy, muddy road.

We think of horse drawn coaches as being used on roads for hundreds of years, but in fact the very first coach to be built in England was only constructed in 1555. The idea received royal approval when Mary I acquired one the following year, but Elizabeth I's coach was actually imported from the Netherlands. By the seventeenth century, however, everything was beginning to change. Coaches and carriages were being built in considerable numbers, and coaches for hire began to appear on London's streets. This caused consternation among the Thames watermen, who had been used to a virtual monopoly for moving citizens around, ferrying them across the river, and taking them for trips up and down the tideway. John Taylor, the waterman poet (1580-1635), was quite happy for royalty and the nobility to ride in carriages but was furious that ordinary citizens now seemed to expect to do so as well.

> Yet tis not fit that every Whore of Knave,
> And fulsome Madam and new scurvy Squires,
> Should jolt the streets in pompe, at their desire:
> Like great triumphant Tamberlanes, each day,
> Drawn with the pamper'd Jades of Belgia.
> That almost all the streets are choak'd out-right,
> Where men can hardly passe from morne till night.

But Taylor was fighting a losing battle. The Tudors had tried to contain London within the old city walls, but expansion was inevitable. At the end of the sixteenth century, for example, Huguenot refugees from the Netherlands, escaping religious persecution, established a thriving silk weaving industry at Spitalfields, outside the city walls. The seventeenth century saw significant changes. What had once been pasture called Leicester Fields was built on to create Leicester Square, developed in 1631 by the Earl of Leicester. Bloomsbury Square and St. James's Square were added in the 1660s, a time which also saw the destruction of a vast swathe of the city in the Great Fire of September 1666. John Evelyn and Christopher Wren both presented plans for rebuilding on a grand scale, with wide, straight streets and an embankment along the Thames. The plans were largely thwarted by the urgent needs of the tradesmen whose livelihood had been destroyed and were anxious to build again as soon as possible to get back into business. A great opportunity was lost, but developments continued throughout the rest of the century, with a series of fashionable squares being added – Golden Square, Grosvenor Square, Berkeley Square, Red Lion Square and Kensington Square had all been completed by 1700. The inexorable growth of London had begun and the distances between the various parts were increasing. Where once the wealthy were happy to walk from place to place, now they preferred someone else to get them there. One of the first means on offer was the sedan chair, introduced to London by Sir Saunders Duncombe in 1664. It was basically an ornate box slung between two poles, with a door at the front to allow a passenger in. It was then picked up by two chairmen who set off to take the occupant to their destination. It was, in effect, London's first taxi service. One feature of the chair was the hinged top. In an age when ladies went in for elaborately piled hair styles and hats sprouting tall feathers, this was an essential if the occupants were not to appear sadly bedraggled at the end of the journey. The sedan chair was very popular, but for the gentry there was nothing quite so good as owning one's own carriage and hiring one's own coachman.

Coach development really began in the late seventeenth century, with the introduction of a simple coach suspended from the

The early nineteenth century saw a new neo-classical style of thoroughfare being developed. This is Regent's Street as it appeared after completion in 1825, looking much as it does today, apart from the cobbled road surface.

Cruikshank's typically sardonic look at a sedan chair. The passers-by have to shelter under umbrellas while the lady in the chair rides in style.

wheeled frame by leather straps. Although this type of carriage helped ease out the bumps, like its predecessor the whirlicote, it still had the same disadvantage of swaying nauseatingly. The idea of providing some type of springing for a coach is thought to have originated in France, but a patent for a simple spring was taken out in England in 1625. The first steel springs, simply C-shaped strips of tempered steel, came into use in the 1660s. Samuel Pepys wrote in his London diary for 5 September 1665 that he had seen a new type of vehicle:

> After dinner came Colonel Blunt in his new chariot, made with springs; as that was of wicker, wherein a while since we rode at his house. And he hath rode, he says now his journey, many miles in it with one horse, and out-drives any coach, and out-goes any horse, and so easy, he says. I went into it to try it, and up the hill to the heath, and over the cart-ruts and found it pretty well, but not so easy as he pretends.

Few devices did more to improve the comfort of a ride in a carriage than the introduction of elliptical springs such as these.

Pepys, alas, gives no details of this carriage, but wickerwork was still being used for some carriages in the eighteenth and early nineteenth centuries. We are fortunate that one very competent artist, William Henry Pyne, took the trouble to record many aspects of life in Britain with great accuracy in sketches and engravings in the first decade of the nineteenth century, including many illustrations of roads and vehicles, some of which are reproduced here. They were published in a volume '*Microcosm*' with text by C. Gray. One of these shows an open wickerwork carriage, known as a 'Sociable'. As designs advanced, comfort was improved by the introduction of more effective springs in the eighteenth century, culminating in the elliptical spring, consisting of multi-layered strips, with upward and downward curving sections joined together. This arrangement cam be seen very clearly in the illustration of a carriage spring on p.26. It is not so very different from the leaf spring used in a modern motor car. The final refinement of attaching the reinforced body directly onto springs mounted on the axles was patented by Obadiah Elliot of Lambeth in 1804. The growing popularity of carriages of all kinds saw large numbers of coach builders setting up in London and working throughout the eighteenth and nineteenth centuries, developing coaches in a great variety of different styles.

This open wickerwork carriage with postillion was very appropriately known as a 'sociable'. Another Pyne illustration.

One of the most popular carriages was the Clarence, named after the Duke of Clarence for whom the first coach was built in the 1830s. One of its distinctive features was the way in which the lower part of the body was cut away at the back, so that the seats were directly above the springs of the rear axle. A somewhat sturdier version was built by Robinson of Mount Street for Lord Brougham. Carriages of this type were also to take the name of the first owner, and the brougham was later developed into the growler, an early form of London cab.

The coach builders worked almost exclusively in wood, buying in metal parts and going to specialists such as wheelwrights for components. The coach body was their speciality and private owners expected a high standard of workmanship, more comparable to that of cabinet makers than the work of jobbing carpenters. Paint work was immaculate, and often carried decoration, and if the owner had such a symbol of nobility, then his coat of arms would be sure to appear on the side. The carriage was very much the status symbol of the day and was subject to changes in fashion, so that for a time if one wanted to keep up with the latest ideas, one's coach would be mounted on unnecessarily large wheels, even though the owner had to use a little step ladder to clamber up into it, which must have been quite a problem for ladies in voluminous dresses. Jane Austen more than once turned her acute eyes on the pretentiousness of carriage owners, whether it was the wonderfully pompous

A Brougham carriage, so called because it was first made for Lord Brougham. It was unusual in having a glazed front window.

clergyman, Mr Collins, boasting of the splendour of the vehicle of his patroness, Lady Catherine de Bourgh in *Pride and Prejudice*, or the boorish Thorpe in *Northanger Abbey* telling everyone what a splendid horse he had and what a fine gig, when inevitably it turned out that his fine steed was not quite the speedy beast he had declared it to be. A planned trip from Bath to Bristol had to be abandoned, because it was too slow, though Thorpe, of course, blamed it on the other driver and his horse. 'My horse would have trotted to Clifton within an hour, if left to himself, and I have almost broke my arm with pulling him in to that cursed broken-winded jade's pace.'

One coach has a grandeur that would have satisfied the most egotistic emperor, but was, in fact, built for the Lord Mayor of London in 1757. Before that, the Lord Mayor had used hired coaches, but Sir Charles Asgill decided that the office needed something more dignified. The coach itself was built in 1757 by Joseph Berry of Leather Lane, but the ornate decoration of gilded wood was designed by Sir Robert Taylor, an architect and sculptor, in a style that can best be described as Rococo. The painted panels were the work of Giovanni Cipriani, a Florentine painter who had settled in England in 1755. He was later to become one of the founding members of the Royal Academy. They are allegorical, representing such noble themes as faith, hope and charity as well as the City's coat of arms. Although there have been essential repairs over the years, such as replacing the wheels, it looks today almost exactly as it did when used for Sir Charles Asgill's inauguration. It appears annually in the Lord Mayor's Parade.

One of the earliest treatises on coach building was written by William Felton and published in 1794. He had his own coach works at Leather Lane, Holborn, but he was quick to praise the work of John Hatchett of Long Acre, next to Covent Garden. He wrote that all the improvements of the previous twenty years had been down to his efforts: 'To him every coach maker is indebted as at present they seldom build without copying his designs.' There were a number of other leading manufacturers in London, including Barker & Co in Chandos Street. One young man who came to Barker's as an apprentice was Samuel Hobson, who was to become one of the most famous and influential of all London coach makers. George Thrupp wrote in 1877 that 'he may truly be said to have improved and remodelled every sort of carriage which came under his notice, especially as regards the artistic form of body and

The Lord Mayor of London's state coach, originally built in 1757, is believed to be the oldest state coach still in use anywhere in the world.

carriage.' He had set up his own business in Long Acre in about 1815, but although his carriages were a great success, he was, like many innovators, a poor business man. He sold out to Peters & Sons in 1837, who continued to use his designs.

William Felton, who had praised Hackett for innovation, was himself involved in what was the most startlingly innovative carriage of the early years. The carriage he was asked to build was not to be pulled by horses but driven by steam.

Steam engines were first developed to drain water from mines. The earliest versions, developed by Thomas Newcomen, were known as atmospheric engines, simply because they partly relied on air pressure to make them work. The pump rods were hung from one end of an overhead beam, pivoted at its centre. At the other end, was a piston in a cylinder. Steam was injected below the piston, then condensed by spraying with water, creating a vacuum. Air pressure forced the piston down, lifting the rods at the opposite end of the beam. Pressure equalized, the rods dropped again and the whole cycle could be repeated. It was a system that used a vast amount of fuel, as the piston was constantly cooled and reheated. The answer was found by James Watt, who used a separate vessel to condense the steam. But heat was still lost through the open top of the cylinder. The next step changed the steam engine radically. He closed the top of the cylinder, and instead of air pressure, used steam pressure. He no longer needed the weight of pump rods to pull down one end of a beam, as the piston could be pushed in both directions. Watt, however, was adamant about one thing. Steam pressure should always be low; if you needed more power, then build a bigger engine – and the engines were massive. Watt had a monopoly that ensured that no one could build an engine with a separate condenser without his permission – and without paying him a fee.

A young Cornish engineer, Richard Trevithick, had different ideas. He realized that if he used high pressure steam, he did not need to condense it at all. He began to develop a small, but powerful, portable engine, that could be towed to where it was needed by a horse. He then began to wonder why a horse was needed at all. Why not build an engine that could drive itself along? On Christmas Eve, 1801, his first experimental road locomotive went puffing triumphantly up Camborne Hill, followed by an excited Cornish crowd. Four days later, Trevithick and friends set off for another jaunt on the engine, but along the way they hit a watercourse and the vehicle overturned. The party decided to make the best of it, by heading for a nearby inn to cheer themselves up. Unfortunately, no one had thought to dowse the fire in the firebox, and while they were still enjoying themselves, the engine blew up. Trevithick was not too dismayed. It was always a prototype, built to see if a self-propelling vehicle would work. He could now go ahead with his great plan to build a steam powered passenger coach that he would demonstrate on the streets of London. The engine was to be built in Cornwall, but it was now that he turned to Felton to supply the coachwork.

The coach was a roomy affair, capable of holding eight people, but was strangely ungainly. The actual coach body was conventional, but was high above the ground, as it needed to be to make space for the engine underneath. This had a horizontal cylinder and the piston was connected to a cranked axle on the rear wheels. These were 8ft in diameter, but at the front of the carriage, instead of a pair of

A replica of Richard Trevithick's steam carriage in Leather Lane, Clerkenwell outside the former premises of William Felton, who made the coachwork for the original. A plaque was being unveiled to mark the event.

wheels, was a small wheel steered by a tiller. Unlike a conventional carriage, because the rear axle was cranked, it was completely unsprung. It must have seemed extraordinary and probably rather terrifying. Trevithick's partner in the enterprise, Andrew Vivian, invited a relative, a sea captain, for a ride. Afterwards he reported that 'he was more likely to suffer a shipwreck on the steam-carriage than on his own vessel.' He never went again.

Trevithick made a number of demonstration runs through the streets of London. John Vivian, Andrew's nephew, wrote a vivid account of a trip in the carriage, which suggests that Captain Vivian was probably quite wise. They made several trips along Tottenham Court Road and round Euston Square. It was on one of these that matters got out of control.

> She was going along five or six miles an hour, and Captain Dick [Trevithick] called out, 'Put the helm down, John!' and before

I could tell what was up, Captain Dick's foot was upon the steering-wheel handle, and we were tearing down six or seven yards of railing from a garden wall. A person put his head from a window and called out, 'What the devil are you doing there! What the devil is that thing!'

Trevithick had hoped to get financial backing that would enable him to develop his idea and build a whole fleet of steam carriages, but London showed no interest and in the end the coach was dismantled and the engine sold. To mark the bicentenary of this event, Tom Brogden of Macclesfield built a replica of this amazing vehicle and brought it up to London for a ceremony in which a plaque was unveiled at the site of Felton's old carriage works. I was invited to make a short speech and the unveiling of the plaque was carried out by a descendant of the engineer, Frank Trevithick Okuno. Afterwards, Frank and I were taken for a ride round Regent's Park and the sight of this strange machine caused as many

The engine at the rear of the Trevithick carriage, which needed the very large wheels to provide clearance for the working parts.

amazed glances as it must have done two centuries before. In spite of the lack of springing, the ride was very comfortable – but we had the advantage of travelling over a far better road surface. It was a wonderful experience and I could only admire the skill of the man at the tiller who controlled such a large vehicle by such a crude device. Had the money been forthcoming, traffic might have been revolutionised at the very start of the nineteenth century, but, as it was, Trevithick made no further attempts to build steam vehicles to run on roads.

Apart from the private carriages, there were also regular coach services from London to other parts of the country. According to Grey, writing in *Microcosm*, the system was begun in 1634, when Captain Baily had a fleet of four coaches, running between London and what was then the village of Hackney. They became known as Hackney cabs, and the name remained in use long after cabs began going to other destinations. The system grew rapidly, though it was controlled by legislation. In 1637, just fifty hackney-coachmen were allowed to operate, but the numbers kept growing until by 1771 there were a thousand. But the stage coach as we think of it was only really developed for long distance travel in the eighteenth century. The finest coaches of all were the mail coaches.

A Pyne drawing of a stage coach with three horses. Coaches of this type were generally used for short journeys from London.

In the eighteenth century, the carrying of letters was a royal monopoly, with the fees being paid on delivery. Although parcels could be carried by anyone, letters had to be entrusted to riders, known as post-boys. This was not a very satisfactory system. Delivery was slow and lone riders were easy to stop and rob – and even murder. John Palmer of Bath was the man who proposed a different system. He pointed out that the new stage coach service introduced between London and Bath did the whole journey in 17 hours as opposed to the post-boys who took 38 hours. A mail coach, he argued, with armed guards would be quicker, cheaper and safer. He also suggested that if the coach owner were also allowed to take passengers and keep the fares, the government wouldn't have to pay to keep the service running. There was some opposition to the idea, particularly from other coach operators. But the real problem was the obstinacy and conservatism of government officials who blithely noted that 'the present arrangement of the post cannot possibly be improved'. Fortunately, there was a change of government, and William Pitt the younger came into power, with a rather more progressive outlook. He over-ruled the Post Office and licensed Palmer to set up a service between Bristol and London via Bath.

A royal mail coach built by John Vidler Jnr. c.1815. This drawing was made by Richard Blake to commemorate the 200th anniversary of the mail coach service.

The first run used an ordinary stage coach with a locked mail chest over the rear axle, an armed guard beside the driver and four inside passengers. Palmer claimed he could beat the best stage time of 17 hours by a full hour. It left Bristol on the afternoon of 2 August 1784 and arrived at the London post office at eight the following morning – in just 16 hours as promised. The return journey was equally successful. There was only one problem. The ordinary coaches were not really designed for fast travel on rough roads, and the wear and tear meant frequent repairs and replacements. The question was – could a coach be designed that would stand up to this rough treatment?

The answer was found in 1787 in the shape of John Besant's Patent Improved Wheel Carriage. It attracted the attention of the Post Office authorities and was supposed to be given a thorough trial. But while Palmer was in France, his deputy Charles Bonner ordered the carriages for the Post Office, anyway. Besant was not himself a coach builder so he went into partnership with the established firm of John Brooks of Long Acre. There was an urgent need for extra finance and one of those who put up money for the enterprise was a stone mason, John Vidler. Bonner suffered a mental breakdown, Besant died, and Vidler became the head of the concern, moving to new premises in Millbank. The Vidler family soon had a monopoly on the supply of mail coaches and their maintenance. The most obvious difference between these coaches and the older stage coaches, was the combination of the locked mail box and guard's seat at the rear of the coach. Monopolies are open to abuse, but the company maintained an exceptionally high standard both in construction and maintenance to ensure that the mail coaches retained their reputation for speed and reliability. The Vidler family lost their monopoly in 1836 and soon after that went out of business, but they had served the country well and had been one of London's most successful coach builders.

We tend to have a rather romantic view of stage coach travel, encouraged in part by the familiar Christmas card scenes of jolly landlords waving off coaches full of contented passengers. But it was not without its problems. Journeys could start early from one of London's coaching inns. The Edinburgh coach, for example, left the Rose and Crown in St John Street at four in the morning, when even the jolliest landlord might be excused for feeling grumpy and passengers were still half asleep. And travellers could not necessarily expect a comfortable ride. Dr Kitchiner, who wrote a travel guide published in 1827, gave this advice. 'If circumstances compel you to ride on the outside of a Coach, put on Two Shirts and two Pairs of Stockings, turn up the collar of your Great Coat and tie a handkerchief around it, and have plenty of dry Straw to set your feet on.' The advice came too late for two travellers on the London to Bath stage in the winter of 1812. When the stage stopped at Chippenham, they were found to have frozen to death.

The alternative to the stage coach was the post chaise. This was a smaller vehicle than a stage coach, but was available for hire and came with one or two men who rode the horses, rather than steering them via reins from a box on the coach. It was an expensive way to travel for an individual but was well priced if two or three were travelling together to share the cost. Grey described the advantages and disadvantages of travel by stage or post chaise.

> Our post-chaise is equally easy, expeditious and safe; we mean safe as to overturning or breaking down; for with respect to those unlicensed assessors of the king's highway, footpads and highwaymen, it is rather dangerous, particularly in the neighbourhood of London. It attracts them, from the idea, that it is generally the more wealthy who travel in it, and at the most, there can seldom be above three in it, while the chance is in favour

A heavily laden stage coach by Pyne. The handles on the roof were all the outside passengers had to hang on by to prevent themselves falling off.

of there being fewer, and that there may be a female or perhaps two. The post-chaise is, therefore, a favourite species of prey with this kind of hunter; and the heaths near London, through which all our great roads run, present them with as favourable a scene as they could wish.

Carriages and post chaises were the vehicles for carrying small parties of the wealthy, but as early as the 1660s there were ideas being developed for moving large numbers of people around city streets in big vehicles. At first, they were unsuccessful, but at the beginning of the nineteenth century, Jacque Laffitte built an eighteen-seat carriage in France. One of his customers ran the vehicles to take passengers to his bathing establishment on the outskirts of Nantes. En route it passed a local grocer's shop called Omnès and, as a pun on the name, the vehicle became known as the Omnès Omnibus. The name stuck and the omnibus was born.

The man responsible for developing the omnibus in Britain was George Shillibeer. He was born in London in 1797 and after serving briefly as a midshipman in the navy, joined Hatchetts in Long Acre to learn the trade of coach building. In 1820 he moved to Paris, where he began developing wide-bodied omnibuses to carry up to twenty-four passengers on the inside of the coach. The coaches proved extremely popular, and he might have remained in France if he had not received a request from a Quaker girls' school in Stoke

A post chaise. These carriages could be hired and instead of a driver on the coach, they had a postillion to ride in front.

Newington, asking him to build a vehicle for the girls. He accepted the commission and built the first school bus. It was well received and Shillibeer decided to return to London to build up a fleet of omnibuses that would run on a regular route with a timetable and designated bus stops.

The first omnibus went into service on 4 July 1829, running from Paddington to the Bank of England in the city. Paddington was not yet a railway terminus but was a rapidly developing suburb. There were four services a day in each direction, and fares ranged from a shilling for the full journey to sixpence for going just part of the way. The fare for the full journey is roughly equivalent to what one would pay today for the same journey by tube. The vehicles looked very attractive and were manned by smartly uniformed staff.

Most stage coaches started their journeys at coaching inns. One of the few survivors is the magnificent galleried George Inn at Southwark.

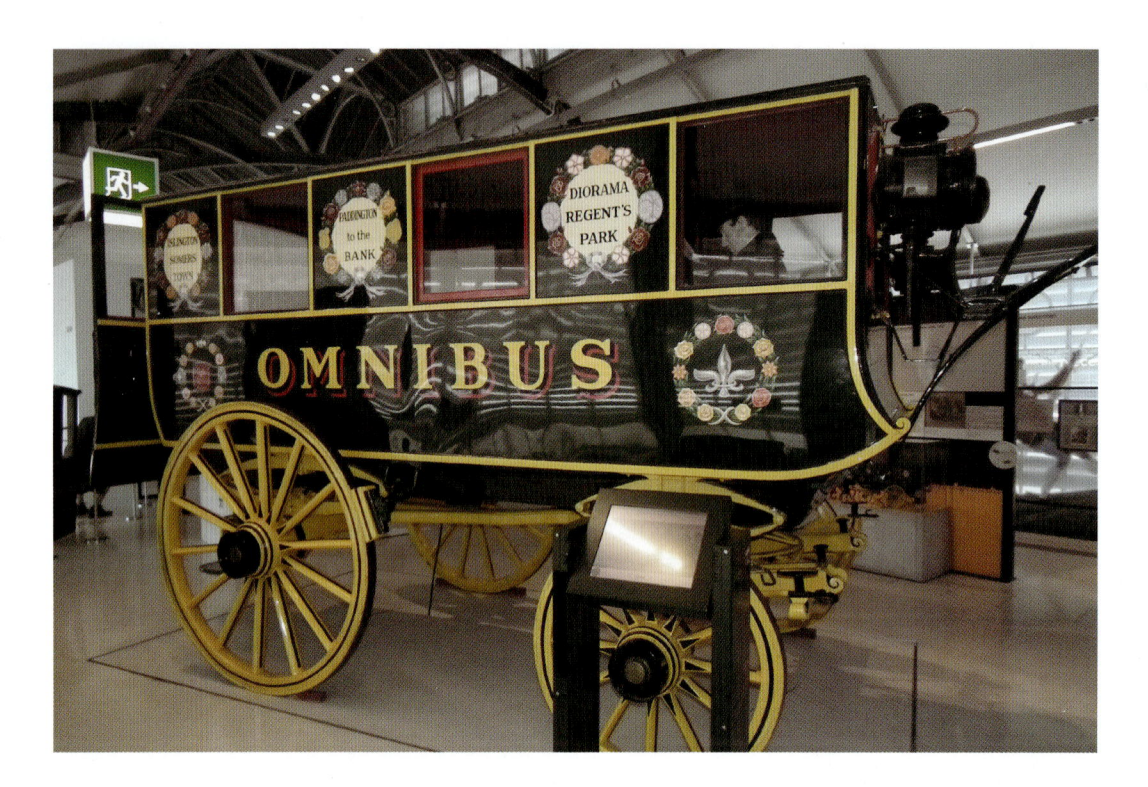

A replica of the Shillibeer horse-drawn omnibus that began running in 1829, taking city workers between Paddington and the Bank of England in 1829.

Unlike the stage coaches of the day, where only the rich travelled inside, and others perched on top, everyone got an inside seat, even if they were only narrow benches. The *Morning Post* gave a very favourable review to the new service but pointed out its one serious disadvantage. It was drawn by three horses, harnessed abreast, which made it difficult to manoeuvre in narrow London streets. It was a problem that could be solved if horses were replaced by steam power.

The first experimental steam coach was designed by Julius Griffith of Brompton, Middlesex in 1821. He went, almost inevitably, to that great engineer Joseph Bramah to get the machine constructed. It was a curious affair. Basically, it was a steam powered flat cart, with the engine and boiler sat above the rear axle and driving the rear wheels through gearing. On top of this was a conventional body, similar to that of a stage coach, mounted on springs. A twopenny newspaper, the *Limbard's Mirror*, gave it an enthusiastic review, claiming that it could travel at five miles an hour for twenty hours and declared that Griffith 'deserved well of his country and mankind'. Alas, their optimism proved unfounded. The boiler proved hopelessly inadequate, and the carriage never managed more than a few short practice runs. The experiment was abandoned. There is, however, some evidence that among those who came to see the device was Walter Hancock, who was to have far more success in developing the steam omnibus.

Hancock was born at Marlborough, where his father was a cabinet maker and timber merchant – a useful combination. He, however, trained as a jeweller and watchmaker and eventually set up in business on his own. He might have continued concentrating on that business if his brother Thomas had not developed an interest in a material that was just starting to find limited use in Britain – rubber. The manufacturing process was very wasteful and small off cuts were simply being scrapped. Thomas decided to try and use these pieces by reuniting them, at first by treating them with chemicals and, when that failed, by machine. He built a masticator, a shredding machine that he expected would turn the rubber into granules. Instead, much to his surprise, it turned out solid, homogeneous rubber. He now needed a factory and someone with mechanical aptitude to help build and design the necessary machinery. He turned to Walter and they established a factory at Stratford in East London. This gave Walter access to a workshop and the opportunity to develop his ideas for a steam carriage. He was convinced an engine needed to be very light, so instead of the conventional iron cylinder and piston, he used two stout canvas bags made impermeable by the addition of rubber, which were alternately filled with steam and exhausted and able to withstand pressures up to 60 pounds per square inch. The system was not a success, largely because the boiler proved inefficient. He wrote his own account of how he developed the steam carriage in a book published in 1836, throughout which he rather confusingly talks of himself in the third person:

> Although the experiments demonstrated the inefficiency of his new engine as a locomotive agent, they left on his mind a strong conviction, that the application of steam power to the propulsion of carriages on common roads was decidedly a practical object. The great and essential desideratum seemed to him to be – a boiler that while it would generate steam rapidly and produce a sufficient and continuous supply, should occupy but little space, be of small weight (comparatively speaking), harmless, if it should burst, simple in its construction and inexpensive in its manufacture; to construct such a boiler became now, therefore, his chief study.

He succeeded in devising his boiler that consisted of a set of vertical, narrow water chambers, joined together by iron stays. The hot gases from the fire passed between the plates, which had some 85 square feet of heating surface supplied by a six foot square grate. The fire was fed with coke, a smokeless fuel that avoided polluting the city streets – though London was already fairly well covered with smoke and soot from countless coal fires. The boiler proved very efficient and quite safe, even when things went wrong – on one trip, the boiler actually burst and none of the passengers were even aware of what had happened.

The first experiments with the canvas bags were quickly abandoned in favour of the more usual piston and cylinder, but at first Hancock used oscillating cylinders set either side of the single front wheel. The first carriages went into service between London and Brighton, but the London and Brighton Steam Carriage Company that was formed in 1832 never went into business, so the carriage, known as *Infant II*, was used to make several trips from the Stratford works. The best known of the Hancock engines was *Enterprise*. This had a fixed, two-cylinder vertical engine set in a separate compartment at the rear of the vehicle. The drive was via a chain to the rear axle, protected from the mud of the road by a shield. It was a fourteen-seat omnibus and was built for the London and Paddington Steam Carriage Company and was designed to follow the same route earlier worked by the Shillibeers. It was agreed that this was an experiment and that if successful, Hancock would manufacture more vehicles for the company. With Hancock himself in charge, the omnibus made regular runs between Paddington and Bank, recording speeds up to 16 miles an hour. It never experienced the trouble negotiating the streets that had plagued the Shillibeers.

Everything should now have been straightforward. *Enterprise* was duly handed over and Hancock waited for the orders. The company, however, proved duplicitous, and built an omnibus of their own, largely based on the Hancock, but with enough small variations to make it appear at least to be an entirely new model. The scheme backfired; the new model was a failure, and Hancock was able to buy his original machine back and carry on building. He continued to make vehicles that ran services in the London area. On one memorable occasion one of the omnibuses was used to take the Stratford cricket team and supporters to a match in Epping, with a total of 32 passengers. The Hancock omnibuses thrived for a time, but one had a name that would certainly not inspire confidence in a

ROADS, CARRIAGES AND OMNIBUSES • **43**

Walter Hancock's steam omnibus ran on the same route as the Shillibeer. It was successful, but the company that ran it treated the inventor badly, and he lost a great deal of money on the venture.

A modern working replica of the Hancock omnibus, built by Tom Brogden, who also built the Trevithick engine, seen here at the Beamish open-air museum: riding in it turns out to be very smooth and comfortable.

modern traveller – it was called *Autopsy*. However, the steam omnibus service never achieved great popularity and horses provided the motive power for much of the nineteenth century traffic in London. By the middle of the nineteenth century, there were many different companies offering omnibus services throughout London.

Moving from the Georgian to the Victorian era, one vehicle seems to epitomise London transport at that time – the hansom cab. The inventor of this vehicle was not an engineer or coach builder but an architect, Joseph Hansom. He was born in York in 1803, where his father was a builder. He set up in business with another young architect, Edward Welsh, in 1827 and in 1831, they received a hugely important commission to design a new town hall for Birmingham. Very rashly, they stood surety for the builder should the project be late or go over budget. The story of large projects is littered with accounts of estimates proving to be wildly over optimistic, and this one was no exception. The sad result was

This *Punch* cartoon of 1828 by Henry Alkens shows an unlikely array of steam vehicles he thought might soon be seen in the Whitechapel Road.

that the company was declared bankrupt, and they had to leave it to others to complete the project. That was the end of the project, but Hansom had far more success working on his own, and enough spare time to think about how a better carriage could be designed for city streets. He called it the 'Patent Safety Cab' and the patent itself was awarded in December 1834.

It was a light vehicle, carried on two large wheels of just over 8ft in diameter. It was designed to be worked with just one horse, and the driver sat at the back on a high seat looking over the top of the cab roof. It could hold two passengers in comfort, and they communicated with the driver by means of a trap door in the cab roof. The front of the vehicle was open but a leather curtain was provided that could be wrapped round the passengers' legs, not just to keep them warm but to save them being spattered by mud. Although we think of it as synonymous with nineteenth century London, it was actually built in Hinckley, Leicestershire. It was immensely popular and by 1889 it was estimated that London had 7,500 hansoms on the streets. One might have expected Hansom to have made a fortune, and he probably thought he had when he sold his interest in the patent for £10,000. Sadly, he only ever received £300 of the amount due. He did, however, go on to have a successful architectural career, designing a number of splendid Catholic churches.

The streets of nineteenth century London were crowded with horse drawn vehicles, which brought with them the inevitable problem of vast quantities of horse droppings. This was the age of full length, sweeping dresses for women – not the ideal accompaniment to a world dominated by dung. But where there is a problem, there is usually a solution. In this case, the answer was to be found in crossing sweepers, usually young children, prepared to clear the way for wealthy pedestrians in exchange for a few coppers. They were to be kept busy until the hansom cabs finally gave way to the motor taxis of the twentieth century.

There was one other important change in the capital that made travelling a good deal safer – the introduction of gas lighting. William Murdoch was a Scottish engineer, employed by Boulton & Watt to supervise the installation of steam engines in Cornwall – and to attempt to prevent anyone trying to build an engine that infringed their patent. In his spare time, he began experimenting with ways in which the gas from burning coal could be used for lighting. The gas, methane, was of course all too well known to coal miners as fire damp, which was the cause of many explosive

The Hansom cab seems today to be the quintessential vehicle of Victorian London. The cab, however, was manufactured in Birmingham.

The proliferation of horse-drawn vehicles on the streets inevitably made them decidedly unsavoury. Children made a few pennies by sweeping a clean path over the road to keep ladies' and gentlemens' shoes clear of the mire.

disasters. What Murdoch had to do was find a way to produce the gas efficiently and with a bright flame. The answer he came up with was to burn the coal in a closed iron tube with a carefully controlled supply of air. The gas then had to be washed to remove obnoxious smells by treating with quicklime. The by-products of the process were tars and coke. At first Boulton & Watt were not interested in developing his idea, but he returned to their Soho works in Birmingham in 1798, and in 1802, he arranged for a celebration of the Peace of Amiens, by illuminating the entire works with 2,600 gas lights. The idea was soon taken up, first in a private house, then in a cotton mill at Salford.

Then a competitor appeared. Friedrich Winzer saw a display of gas lighting devised by Philippe Lebon and decided to try and set up his own gas lighting company in London, under the Anglicised name of Francis Winser. He attempted to get parliament to grant him a monopoly for lighting London. The attempt failed as Murdoch was able to establish that he was the inventor of gas lighting. Winser was allowed to start a company on a limited scale, but there was no enthusiasm for the product, even when he offered to install lights for free. Eventually, Samuel Clegg, Murdoch's assistant, went to London to take over the Winser company, installing new plant on the lines developed at Soho. The company was given a new name – The London and Westminster Chartered Gas Light and Coke Company. By 1823, a Parliamentary Committee formally declared that 'much benefit' would derive from lighting London's streets by gas. A new era of well-lit streets had finally arrived in the capital. There is, however, another source of methane – human waste. For a time, an area in the Strand was lit by lighting gas from the sewers.

There were several reasons why London traffic increased so rapidly throughout the eighteenth and nineteenth centuries. A growing population meant that the city was spreading out to swallow up old settlements, which were now merely suburbs. Road improvements made travel both far easier and a great deal more comfortable. There was a third factor, which we haven't touched on yet. The Thames had for centuries only been crossed in the whole London area by the single, ancient bridge. That began to change at the end of the eighteenth century and that is the subject of the next chapter.

A Rowlandson cartoon showing a variety of citizens staring at the gas lights that had just been installed in Pall Mall in 1807.

Chapter Three

Crossing the Thames

It was to take five centuries before a second bridge joined London Bridge to cross the Thames in the London area. A proposal was put forward to the House of Commons in 1671 for a bridge at Fulham, but it was opposed by the City of London, largely because the authority enjoyed a very useful revenue from licensing watermen. The argument they put forward, however, was quite odd; such a bridge would extend the city's boundaries and 'England itself shall be as nothing'. Quite why extending London would lessen England remains a mystery, but the plan was thrown out. Half a century later, London was to get its new bridge, largely, it appears, because a ferryman was in the pub enjoying a pint instead of waiting for clients who wanted to cross the river. Fortunately for Londoners, the gentleman who was kept waiting at Putney was a man shortly to become prime minister, Robert Walpole. When a proposal was put forward for a bridge at Putney, Walpole was an enthusiastic supporter. The matter was agreed, but there were important interests to pacify and pay off. Fulham Palace was home to the Bishop of London, while Putney was part of the estate of the Manor of Wimbledon owned by the Duchess of Marlborough. Both received compensation for the loss of revenue from the ferry service. Even that was not enough. The new bridge was to be a toll bridge, and both the Bishop and the Duchess, together with their staff, were allowed to cross for free. £62 was set aside to be paid annually to the children of watermen.

This was an important venture, and it was financed by selling thirty shares at £1,000 each. The investors made sure that competition could be controlled by purchasing the old ferry for £8,000. The bridge was built entirely of timber, joining Fulham High Street at one side with Putney High Street on the other, but because they were not directly opposite each other, the bridge was built with a kink in it at the Putney end. The overall length was 786 feet with 26 spans. The width was just 24 feet, which led to congestion, but there were triangular platforms above each of the piers to enable pedestrians to get out of the way of coaches and carriages.

There was a large toll gatehouse at the Fulham end, which also held the company offices, and a smaller tollhouse at Putney. The chances of avoiding payment were slim. If anyone managed to slip past at one end, a bell was rung and he or she was nabbed on the far side. It was a success for the investors, bringing in a very considerable income, especially after it started to be regularly used by stage coaches. On the other hand, it was, judging by the illustration on above, a somewhat ramshackle affair, and was frequently damaged by boats and barges. However, it continued in use from its opening in 1729 right up to 1886, when a new bridge was constructed upstream from the old. Designed by Joseph Bazalgette, it was a much more solid stone construction, 44 foot wide and with just five arches. It is an elegant structure that gets seen by millions every year, as the starting point for the Oxford and Cambridge boat race.

The original wooden Putney bridge: an illustration from William Armstrong's book *The Thames* published c.1870.

A second timber bridge was constructed at Battersea, but that had not been what the promoters had wanted. Earl Spencer had acquired the Manor of Battersea and formed the Battersea Bridge Company with the aim of building a splendid stone bridge across the river. The hoped-for investment never materialised, so a cheaper timber bridge had to be built instead. It turned out to be a false economy. With nineteen arches, it proved difficult to

The present
Putney bridge, designed by Joseph Bazalgette.

negotiate and was frequently severely damaged so that profits from tolls were soon swallowed up by costly repairs. It does have one historical distinction as the first London bridge to be lit at night, using oil lamps. It was considered rather picturesque, and attracted a number of artists, including Turner and Pissarro, but the most famous painting was by Whistler, titled 'Nocturne Blue and Gold – old Battersea Bridge'. It was far too impressionistic for the British public of 1877, and the critic John Ruskin described it as 'flinging a pot of pain in the public's face'. Whistler sued for libel and won but it was a distinctly hollow victory: he received damages of just one farthing.

The timber bridges were already something of an anachronism in the eighteenth century and the first new stone bridge had been a long time coming. As early as 1664, a proposal had been made for a bridge at Westminster, but it faced precisely the same strong opposition as the Fulham bridge. The idea was brought forward again in 1721 but with exactly the same result. The scheme, however, had the backing of the Earl of Pembroke and in 1736 parliament

CROSSING THE THAMES • 51

Battersea bridge was the last bridge in the London area to be constructed from timber. It was not a great success and was soon replaced; another illustration from *The Thames*.

Whistler's famous painting of Battersea bridge, which resulted in a lawsuit for libel, when it was described as a mere daub.

finally agreed that a bridge was essential, though once again the other interests had to be bought off – the Archbishop of Canterbury received compensation of £21,000 for loss of revenue from the ferry. It was originally planned to have stone piers, but with a timber deck. Work got under way, but with just two piers completed, the Thames froze over. As it turned out, instead of a misfortune this turned out to be a benefit. The plans for the timber structure were abandoned and it was decided that the whole structure would be of masonry. The new bridge was to have been quite ornate, decorated with statues. Canaletto painted the bridge, but as it had not yet been completed, he added in all the decorative features that were on the plan. In fact, most of them were never realised. This did not prevent several artists who couldn't be bothered to go and see the bridge for themselves, copying the Canaletto. In fact, the bridge had no real need for decoration, as it was a handsome structure. There were, however, problems during construction. The different piers were built under separate contracts and not all were built to the same high standard. As a result, there was some subsidence over the years.

The bridge was opened in 1750 and was able to take three carriages abreast, but the roads leading up to it were the familiar

The first Westminster bridge in a painting by Joseph Farrington of 1789.

London mix of narrow alleys and crowded houses. As a result, there was a wholesale clearance of the old to make way for the new Parliament Street, and at the same time Whitehall was widened. What had once been an area that if not actually a slum was precious close to one, now became home to more handsome buildings. It is doubtful if Wordsworth would have famously written of the view from the bridge – 'Earth hath not anything to show more fair' – if he had arrived a few decades earlier. It remained in use until it was replaced by the present bridge, opened in 1862. Stone had now given way to cast iron and the simple classic to Gothic detailing.

One other masonry bridge was completed in the century. It was promoted by the City of London. Though originally named the William Pitt Bridge after the then prime minister, the elder Pitt, the name was later changed to Blackfriars, as it was near the site of the former monastery. It was designed by the Scottish architect and civil engineer Robert Mylne. He had done the Grand Tour in his younger days and was greatly impressed by the classical architecture of the ancient world, so the bridge was elegantly Italianate in style. Built of Portland stone, it crossed the river on nine elliptical arches, and although it looked very fine, it turned out the workmanship left a great deal to be desired. It opened in 1769 but was so constantly

The present
Westminster bridge, designed by Joseph Cubitt, in which masonry gave way to iron.

under repair that in 1860 it was demolished and replaced by the present bridge, designed by Joseph Cubitt. It resembled the original only in having elliptical arches, but now had just five arches and instead of Portland stone it was constructed from wrought iron.

There were no more bridges built across the river in the eighteenth century, but the old London Bridge was drastically altered. All the buildings that had lined it were removed by 1762, creating a far wider roadway. Even so, it was still a major obstacle to river traffic. A competition was announced in 1799 for designs for a replacement, and one entry was from Thomas Telford. It was "an extraordinary affair", a great cast iron structure stretching for 600 feet across the river in one single arch. Iron bridges were not new. The famous iron bridge over the Severn, that gave the town of Ironbridge its name, had been opened in 1781. This had been followed by an even more imposing bridge across the Wear at Sunderland, again a single iron span but this time 240ft across – then the largest single span ever built. What Telford was proposing was over twice as wide again. The iron master, William Reynolds, whom Telford had worked with before, was enthusiastic. 'I think your plan for the Iron Bridge excellent & do not see the least difficulty in its execution'. Others were altogether more sceptical. In the event it never came to fruition. Modern engineers who have looked at the plan have been equally dubious. Even with the massive abutments that Telford had allowed for, it is doubtful if they could have withstood the thrust from the arch. If it had been built and had remained firm, it would have been the most extraordinary building of the age.

In the event, the design that was finally accepted was by another of the leading engineers of the day, John Rennie. It was a conventional design, with five stone arches built of granite. Work began in 1829 and it was opened for traffic in 1831. Once it was completed, the

Thomas Telford produced this design for a cast iron bridge to replace the old London bridge. It was ambitious but probably impractical.

old bridge was demolished. The main costs were not those for the bridge itself. Because the old bridge remained such a vital link in the London transport system, it had to be kept open while the new was being constructed, which meant that the latter no longer lined up with the former roads. Property had to be bought and demolished to make way for new roads and the approach to the north was named King William Street, after the reigning monarch William IV. Paying for the new roads cost three times as much as the bridge. It was, however, to become London's busiest bridge, and as a result had to be widened in 1896. Even that proved inadequate for the motor traffic of the twentieth century. In 1968 it was put up for sale and was bought by the oil magnate Robert P. McCullough and shipped to Arizona, where it now straddles Lake Havasu, a tribute to the lasting quality of Rennie's design. The present London bridge is unashamedly modern and unadorned, consisting of just three spans of pre-stressed concrete girders.

The nineteenth century was to see a flurry of bridge building across the Thames from Richmond right down to the Pool of London, and it would be very repetitive to describe each one in any sort of detail. Instead, we shall have a look at two types of bridges that first appeared in London during this time, starting with suspension bridges.

Constructing the new London bridge, designed by John Rennie, to replace the medieval structure.

THE NEW LONDON BRIDGE.
As it appeared on Monday August 1st 1831 at the Ceremony of opening by their Majesties.

The grand opening of London Bridge in 1831, attended by the royal family. It remained in use until 1968, when it was removed and now stands over a lake in Arizona.

The idea of a suspension bridge, in which the platform would be hung from iron chains, was first developed at the beginning of the nineteenth century and was made possible by a change in technology. The development of the blast furnace using coke as a fuel had revolutionised iron making, producing iron with a high carbon content – cast iron. This is very strong in compression, but weak in tension, so it is good, for example, for use as a supporting column, but not for suspending weights. The purer form, wrought iron, has exactly the opposite characteristics. It became more widely available thanks to the development of a new kind of furnace, the puddling furnace, which converted cast iron to wrought iron. One man who experimented with using the material was Captain Samuel Brown. As a former naval officer, he was well aware that the vast cables, made from rope and used to hold anchors, were far from ideal, and he developed a system for making anchor chains for the Royal Navy that he patented in 1817. He then went on to develop his chains for suspension bridges. The great advantage of the suspension bridge lies in the fact that because it only relies on chains suspended from towers on either bank, there is no need for arches in the river. Brown built two bridges, each with four suspension chains. One at Berwick had a very short life, having been destroyed in a fierce gale just six months after completion. The other, the Union Bridge over the Tweed, still survives, the world's oldest suspension bridge. Among the engineers who consulted Brown, was Thomas Telford. He was faced with constructing a bridge to cross the Menai Straits and the waterway had to be kept clear for shipping. His suspension bridge provided the answer.

London's first suspension bridge crossed the river at Hammersmith.

The present Hammersmith bridge shows the strong influence of Gothic fashions in its elaborate towers.

The Hammersmith Bridge Company was formed in 1828 and plans were approved by parliament. The engineer was William Tierney Clark, who had started his working life as an apprentice to a millwright but had later gone to the famous ironworks at Coalbrookdale to learn about the metal and its potential uses. Before starting work on the bridge design, he made the trip to Menai and consulted Telford about suspension bridges. The success of that bridge encouraged the company to allow him to build London's first suspension bridge. It was an imposing structure. The eight chains, consisting of wrought iron bars, were anchored to piers on the shore, then passed over 48-foot-high towers. Vertical iron rods were hung from the chains to support a wooden deck, that was topped with granite. The roadway was 689ft long, with a 20ft carriageway and narrow footpaths to either side. As with other bridges, extra cost was involved in building approach roads. As with many early bridges, it proved inadequate for the increased traffic of London and had to be rebuilt. Once again Bazalgette was the chosen engineer. It doubled the width of the roadway to 40 foot and the new towers were in the more elaborate Gothic style favoured by the Victorians.

One of the most famous of Britain's suspension bridges was entrusted to a young engineer, who had just started out in business, working with his father. He was Isambard Kingdom Brunel and the bridge was to cross the Avon gorge at Clifton on the outskirts of Bristol. Unfortunately, the money ran out before it could be completed, and for many years the two supporting towers stood above the river as ungainly stumps. But then he was invited to build another suspension bridge, across the Thames at Hungerford. The design was similar to that of the Hammersmith bridge, but it too was destined to have a short life. Begun in 1841 it was demolished in 1860 to make way for the new railway bridge. There is, however, an interesting quirk to this story. Instead of being sent for scrap, the suspension chains were sent off to Bristol to complete the Clifton bridge Brunel had begun so many years before.

One area that seemed likely to be forever inaccessible for the early bridge engineers was the Thames downstream from London Bridge. This was an area crowded with high masted ships and the fortune of London depended to a very large extent on there being nothing to impede them. But if it was not possible to go over the lower part of the Thames, might it be possible to go under it? The proprietors of the newly formed Thames Archway

Company certainly thought so and in 1805 they received an Act of Parliament authorising them to raise £140,000 in £100 shares and had permission to borrow a further £60,000 if needed to complete a tunnel. One of the most enthusiastic supporters of the idea was a Cornish mining engineer, Robert Vaizie, who bought shares himself and persuaded his family to follow his example. He had carried out test borings and was convinced the scheme was feasible and was the obvious man to take charge. The tunnel was to pass under the Limehouse Reach, and Vaizie simply treated the project as he would have done if opening up a mine – sink a shaft to the correct depth, and then have miners work away from the foot to make the tunnel. It was not to be constructed to the full size. The first stage would be to dig a narrow drift. But things did not go well. At the end of the first year, all that was to be seen for the year's budget was an incomplete shaft, a hundred yards from the riverbank – and no sign of any tunnel. The Company were less than happy and decided to call in two experts to advise them – John Rennie and William Chapman – but the two experts simply disagreed with each other and with Vaizie, so that took things no further. They then decided they needed another competent engineer to work alongside Vaizie. And the man they chose for the job was Richard Trevithick. He and Vaizie were to be placed on an equal footing. It was always in Trevithick's nature to be optimistic, and he greeted this new project with great enthusiasm.

He was to be paid £500 when the drift reached halfway and a further £500 when it reached the other side. He brought in experienced Cornish miners, to work three six-hour shifts, each shift to be worked by three men – the most that could fit into such a confined space. Rails would be laid on the floor of the drift to allow spoil to be brought to the foot of the shaft. He expected the whole job would take nine months. 'I think', he wrote, 'this will be making a thousand pound very easy.' He was soon to discover things would not go quite as planned.

In August 1807, Trevithick wrote that all was going well with the drift, which was 5ft high and 3ft wide at the bottom. There were hints of trouble ahead, however, as he kept encountering what he called 'houses of water', areas in which water had seeped in, mixed with sand and produced quicksand. Three of these had been met, each of them covering an area of about twenty square yards. There was no doubt that progress had improved since Trevithick's arrival, but things were not advancing as rapidly as everyone had hoped and expected. The company directors reasoned that things had not gone well when Vaizie had sole control, but as they were now going better, any faults must lie with Vaizie. He was sacked, which was a terrible blow to the man who had spent years on the project.

The decision seemed to be vindicated as work went on twice as fast as before, but in November they hit solid rock. If this had been a mine, they would simply have drilled holes, filled them with gunpowder and blasted it away. But they were too near the river bed, so the only option was to break it by hand with chisels and wedges. Soon after that they discovered a patch of sandy clay with oyster shells embedded in it, which suggested they were far closer to the river bed than they expected. The men moved cautiously and for a time they were faced with a gooey mess of quicksand that kept oozing into the workings, so extra care had to be taken in shoring up the drift, so as not to leave any gaps. Then on 26 January 1808, the roof began to break up and water flooded in. Trevithick's wife Jane, who had only just arrived in London from Cornwall, was horrified to see her husband arriving home covered in clay and without his shoes and hat. Fortunately, all the men had got out safely.

The hole was patched up and the workings pumped dry again. The men continued working and, by 2 February, Trevithick noted that they were now just under the low water mark on the far bank. With just 70 feet to go, the work became almost impossible as sand and water kept rushing into the workings. The directors were dismayed, but Trevithick simply came forward with a new plan for building the tunnel, which he explained in a letter of 28 July 1808.

> The plan I have laid before them is to make a caisson, 50ft long, 30ft wide and as high as from the bottom of the river to high water. It is made of whole balk, the joints caulked tight as a ship. On the caisson is placed an engine for driving the piles and drawing them again, and also for lifting bricks out of the barges, and the stuff out of the caisson into the barges, by a crane worked by an engine. The piles must be driven within this caisson, in every square, and as deep as the bottom of the tunnel. Then remove the earth and construct 50 feet in length of brick tunnel; then remove the caisson, draw the piles and refix them 50 feet further on in the river, and add another piece to the tunnel, and so on, until the whole is finished …

The first plan was for a tunnel of 11 feet in diameter, for foot passengers only, and was to be 14 feet lower than this present plan.

This plan is two tunnels side by side, 12 feet diameter, each to have a waggon road of 8 feet wide, and a foot-path of 4 feet wide; one tunnel to admit persons going forward, the other backward, so as to prevent mischief in passing.

This was certainly a bold plan, and Trevithick's own sketch of the proposed system is reproduced below. But although Trevithick claimed his caisson would take up no more space than one 40-ton ship at anchor, the Thames authorities were never likely to view the idea with much enthusiasm. The directors were always nervous and called in yet more experts to investigate the whole project and to Trevithick's considerable disappointment, the decision was taken that the whole thing was impossible. Work stopped and the project was abandoned. Not everyone involved, however, lost faith. Trevithick's involvement was over, but two decades later another great engineer was to take up the challenge.

Marc Brunel, as a young man with Royalist sympathies, had been forced to flee revolutionary France. He had gone first to America,

A sketch by Richard Trevithick for the Thames tunnel. On the left, a caisson is being lowered to the riverbed and piling driven in to allow excavation to start. On the right is the double-bore tunnel between the piling and a drift tunnel underneath for drainage. His tunnel was never completed.

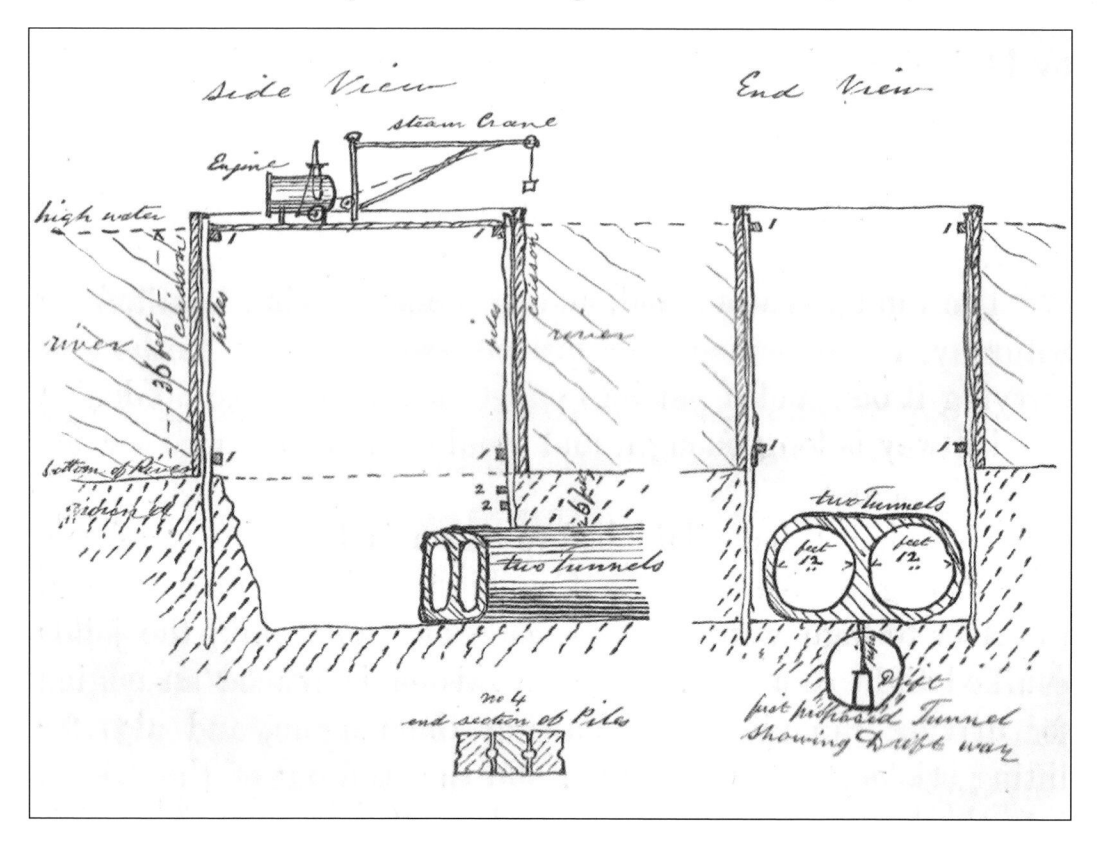

and then to Britain where he quickly established a reputation as an inventive engineer. He designed machinery for making blocks – the pulleys used for manipulating rope on sailing ships. It was arguably one of the world's earliest mass production schemes, as he had broken down the manufacture into different parts, each process carried out by a different machine. His block-making mill was established at the Naval dockyard at Portsmouth. He went on to provide more new machinery for the Admiralty. In a busy life, he was also invited to submit a design for a bridge over the River Neva. He produced his design, but also began to think about the idea of tunnelling under the river rather than striding across it. This led him to take out a patent for a new way of tunnelling. He described the proposal:

> In the formation of a drift under the bed of a river, too much attention cannot be paid to the mode of securing the operation against the breaking down of the earth. It is on this account that I propose to resort to the use of a casing or cell, intended to be forced forward before the timbering which is generally applied to secure the work …The workman thus enclosed and sheltered may work with ease and perfect security.

One of the directors of the first Thames tunnel company, I.W. Tate, heard about the patent and approached Brunel with the idea of using his idea as the basis for a new Thames tunnel project. Brunel agreed and, by the end of 1823, his plans were ready to put before parliament. The Act was passed in February the following year and authorised the new company to raise the capital by issuing 4,000 £50 shares. Brunel now set about designing what he had first called the 'cell' but was now to become the tunnelling shield. As with the first tunnel, there were to be two bores, to allow uninterrupted travel in both directions. Originally it was intended to be used by both pedestrians and carriages, with approaches between the tunnel and the surface along spiral ramps, much as we use a similar system for some multi-storey car parks. There were to be two shields, one for each bore. Each shield was divided into twelve compartments, 7ft high and 3ft wide, in each of which a miner could work at the face. At the back of the shield was a platform on which bricklayers could work to line the tunnel. Metal plates above the top compartments protected the roof. Inside the compartment was a set of heavy oak boards, known as poling boards, held in place by screws. The miner would remove one board, excavate the ground behind it to a depth of 4½ inches, then replace that board, screw it in place, and remove the next board. Once the whole face had been removed in this way, the shield was moved forward. The shield may literally only have inched along, but it was safe and secure.

The first stage was the sinking of the shaft at Rotherhithe. This was not only intended to give access to the workers, but once the tunnel was completed it would also hold the carriage ramp. It was fifty feet in diameter and had to be sunk to a depth of 42 feet. An iron hoop was built, with the bottom of the rim sharpened to a point. Wooden baulks were placed on top, and a pile driver used to drive it into the ground. This then formed the base on which a brick tower could be erected. As the weight of bricks increases, so the hoop sank ever deeper, and the spoil inside the tower was removed. Work began on 9 March 1825 and was completed on 21 November. The shields were lowered down and work on the actual tunnel got under way.

At first things went well and the tunnel reached the river, 18 feet from the shaft, cutting through solid clay. But after 250 feet of tunnelling, Brunel discovered exactly the problem that had plagued Trevithick but in place of clay, the men came across an ever-changing mixture of sand, quicksand and, in places, solid rock. Inevitably, this slowed everything down. Brunel now had to contend with another problem, a constant stream of criticism from one of the directors, William Smith. However, the rest of the Board continued to support him. Then Armstrong, the resident engineer on site, fell ill, and Marc brought in his son as his replacement. It was the first step on a road that would lead the young Isambard to becoming Britain's most famous engineer.

Early in 1827 it became clear that the ground above the tunnel was very loose. Just how loose was vividly demonstrated, when a boat was sent out and a man with a long iron rod poked it down

A section of the tunnelling shield designed by Marc Brunel. The shield provided protection for the workmen in the different cells and was moved forward as the work progressed.

This advertisement for the opening of the Brunel tunnel, shows the full extent of the shield with its workmen in the diagram on the right.

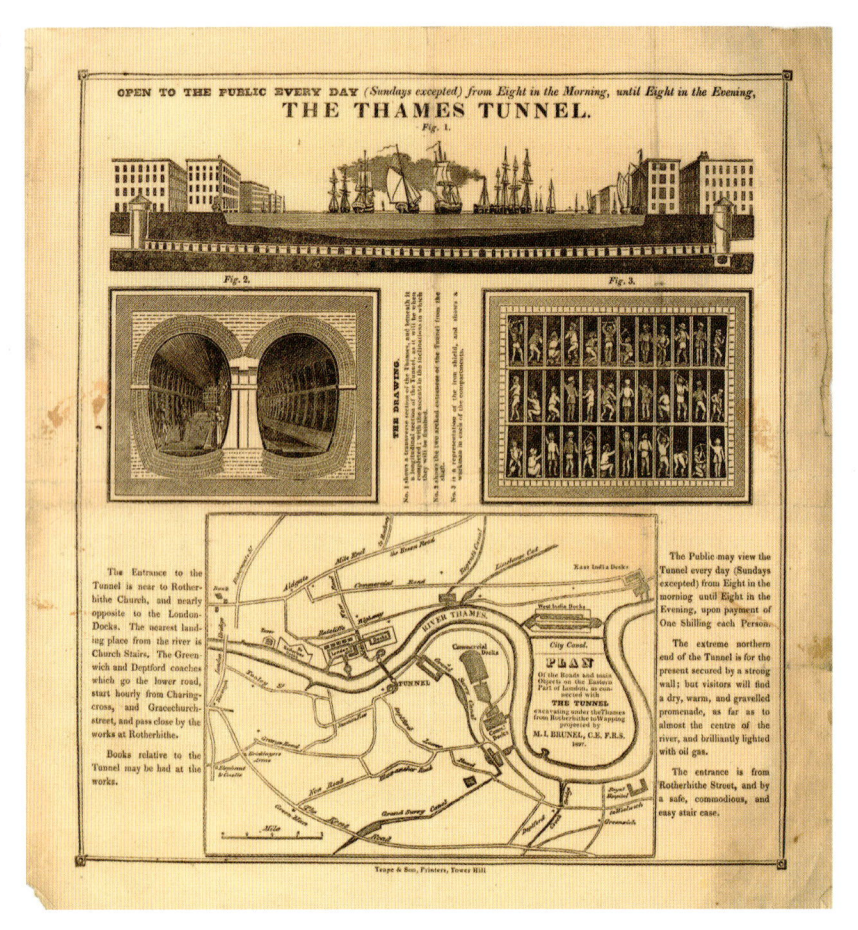

into the riverbed. It went straight down with no effort and hit the top of the shield. It was an ominous sign. On 18 May 1827, the water burst over one of the frames. The engineer Mr Beamish, who shared the job of superintending the works with Isambard and the men, started back up the tunnel towards the shaft. When he reached the foot, he was met by Isambard, and they looked back on a scene of devastation. Beamish described the scene.

> The spectacle that presented itself will not readily be forgotten. The water came on in a great wave, everything on its surface becoming the more distinctly visible as the light from the gas-lamps was more strongly reflected. Frequently a loud crash was heard. A small office, which had been erected under the arch, about a hundred feet from the frames, had burst. The pent air rushed out; the lights were suddenly extinguished, and the noble

work, which only a few short hours before had commanded the homage of an admiring public, was consigned to darkness and solitude.

Miraculously no one was killed, though Isambard had to go to the rescue of one man. The site of the collapse was investigated using a diving bell and the frames were found to be intact. There was, however, a great depression in the riverbed, gouged out by the anchors of countless ships that had come to rest in the river down the years. Eventually, the hole was filled in, though it required 20,000 cubic feet of gravel to make it secure and by November the pumps had cleared away the water. Work could resume. It was decided to hold a grand dinner in the partially opened tunnel to celebrate the restart of work and inspire confidence. It was a sumptuous affair, with the tunnel draped in crimson velvet and the feast accompanied by music from the band of the Coldstream Guards. It turned out to be decidedly premature. Once again, the waters burst in. Isambard was momentarily trapped by a timber that fell across his leg, but he managed to extricate himself and make his way to the foot of the shaft. He had just arrived, when a great surge of water hit him, but instead of carrying him back to a certain death, it threw him up the shaft and out, popping up like a cork from a champagne bottle. He was fortunate: six of the workmen were not and were drowned.

This time, there was to be no restart. Although attempts were again made to plug the hole, and although the men managed to get back into the tunnel, all the extra expense had emptied the coffers. The money had run out. Attempts were made, led by the Duke of Wellington, to raise £200,000 to finish the work. But this was the second attempt to tunnel under the Thames that had failed. Confidence had ebbed away, and only £9,600 was raised. The tunnel entrance was bricked up and that it seemed was the end of the enterprise.

In 1834 a petition to parliament resulted in the Chancellor, Lord Althorp, announcing that the government would support a loan of £240,000 to complete the work. The first task was to remove the old, damaged shield and replace it with a new one. This was a massive operation in all senses of the word. Where the original shield had weighed 80 tons, the replacement was to be a robust 140 tons. It took from the start of work right up to November 1835 to get the old shield out and another four months to get the new

After the flooding of the tunnel during construction, a huge banquet was held to celebrate the restart of work.

one in. Progress was slow but steady, but many of the old troubles returned to plague the workers, with the addition of a new hazard – methane occasionally appeared and alarmingly burst into flame, but without causing any real damage. Another hole appeared as the tunnel edged towards the far shore, and had to be filled in. But with the half-way point passed, it was time to start digging the shaft on the far bank at Wapping. The old problem of loose soil was solved by Marc Brunel – Isambard by now had projects of his own. Before work started on cutting at a new face, the whole shield was jacked forward, compressing the earth in front of it. On 15 December 1841, one of the boards in the shield was removed and instead of compacted earth, the miner found a brick wall. They had reached the Wapping shaft. On 25 March 1848, the tunnel was officially opened with another grand banquet. It was considered one of the wonders of the age, and during the first day thousands of Londoners trooped through it. Sadly, it was not the grand carriageway Brunel had planned. The soaring costs meant that it was only available to pedestrians, with stairs replacing the ramps. However, Queen Victoria and Albert made a visit and for a time its curiosity value brought in the crowds, but as the novelty wore off, the crowds dwindled. It had an unsavoury reputation, and while nobody minded going down the long staircase to reach the tunnel, it was a bit of a slog climbing back to the surface at the other side. It will reappear later in this story, but even if it had never been a success, it had proved its value. The Brunel shield was the basis for many more tunnels that would be built down the years. His was not the last tunnel beneath the river.

The only reason that the expensive and complex business of tunnelling was ever agreed, was to provide a transport route that did not interfere with shipping. But at the end of the nineteenth century, this section of the river was finally crossed by the structure that has become one of London's iconic features – Tower Bridge. The idea was first put forward for consideration by a committee set up by the City of London Corporation in 1876. They launched a public competition to provide a design and from over fifty entries, one was finally selected in 1884. It was a joint proposal from the engineer John Wolfe Barry and the City Architect Sir Horace Jones – the latter was actually one of the selection committee. It has to be said, however, that the selection was sound as this was unquestionably the best engineering solution. It was a hybrid, part suspension bridge, part bascule. The two sections linking the towers to the shore were suspended

The Thames tunnel after its opening in 1848. Although originally intended for use by carriages, shortage of funds made that impossible and it was only used by pedestrians.

by chains, and the central section contained the two lifting bascules. There was also a high-level pedestrian section. Looking at the bridge today, the towers seem little more than supports for the suspension chains, though decked out in true Victorian Gothic style in granite and Portland stone. They are not quite what they seem. The stone is little more than an ornate cladding for a steel frame, and the interesting thing is what happens inside the two tall towers.

There are two steam engines in the towers, but they do not actually move the bascules, that is done by hydraulic power. This form of power

Tower Bridge under construction from a contemporary illustration in *The Engineer*. It shows the basic metal frame that underlies the two towers.

The opening day of Tower Bridge in 1894.

was already in use in the London docks for cranes. The principle is quite simple. If you have a large quantity of water, it will exert pressure and if you allow it to pass down a narrow tube that ends in an object that can move, then it will indeed move. That is why a comparatively feeble human being only has to put his foot on a brake pedal to force a heavy motor car to stop. The steam engines pump water into hydraulic accumulators, each weighing around 100 tons. This means that there is always power available when needed. The water exerts an enormous pressure of 750 pounds per square inch, and when released can raise the bascules weighing around a thousand tons in just a minute and a half. When the bascules drop back into place, they are securely held by two hydraulically operated bolts. The steam engines are now redundant, replaced by electric motors, but the same hydraulic system is still in use. In 1892, the bridge was opened to the public, who get a chance to admire the splendid mechanism, one of the great triumphs of Victorian engineering. There were other crossings both over and under the Thames with the arrival of a new form of transport in the nineteenth century.

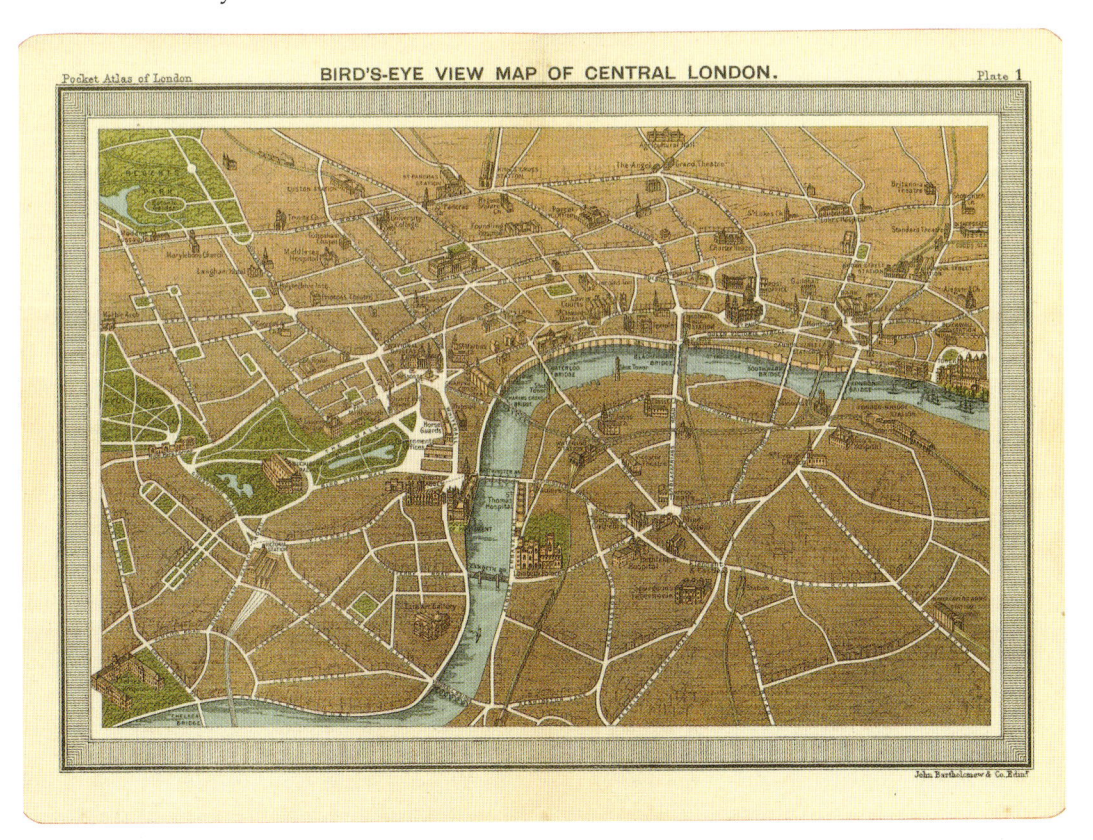

This nineteenth-century bird's eye view shows all the river crossings that existed by that date.

Chapter Four

The Railway Age

Railways came into existence long before the steam locomotive was even dreamed of. The earliest versions had simple wooden rails, along which wagons could be drawn by horses. By the early eighteenth century, the wooden rails were strengthened by iron plates and wagons were fitted with iron wheels. The most important change came in 1767, when special cast iron rails were produced at the famous Darby ironworks at Coalbrookdale in Shropshire. This led to a new generation of tracks, known usually as plateways or tramways. They were mainly constructed by private companies, typically by colliery owners to carry the coal to a navigable river or canal. The rails themselves were L-shaped in cross section, the vertical part keeping the wheels on track. Because they were used by horses, the sleepers which are such a familiar part of modern railway lines would have been no use: one cannot imagine a horse trying to pick its way up such a track. Instead, stone sleeper blocks were used. These were squared stones with a hole drilled in the middle, that was filled with a wooden plug. Parallel lines of these blocks were laid, and the rails fastened on top by metal spikes driven into the wooden plugs. Such a system reached London in 1801, when an Act was passed authorizing the construction of the Surrey Iron Railway to run from the Thames at Wandsworth to Croydon. It has the distinction of being the very first public railway to be authorized by Act of Parliament. It was laid out by the canal engineer William Jessop and its aim was to bring agricultural produce from the country to the capital and to provide coal to the country from the colliers that arrived in the Thames from the north of England. It was opened in 1803 and was sold in 1844 to the London & South Western Railway. Steam locomotives had taken the place of horses, but the old, brittle tramway plates would have collapsed under the weight of an engine. Some of the stone sleeper blocks were salvaged, and I was delighted when, some years ago, when I visited the Young's brewery in Wandsworth to find several of them embedded in the courtyard wall.

While the Surrey Iron Railway was being completed, Richard Trevithick was trying unsuccessfully to interest Londoners in

THE RAILWAY AGE • 71

Stone sleeper blocks to which the rails of the Surrey Iron Railway were once spiked, preserved in the wall of the Young's brewery in Wandsworth.

investing in his steam carriage, a vehicle like a stagecoach, powered by a small engine. One of the problems he never really solved was steering, which in the case of the carriage was a tiller controlling a small front wheel. That was, however, solved for him when he was invited by a Welsh iron master, Samuel Homfray of the Penydarren iron works in Merthyr Tydfil, to build a locomotive to run on his tramway that connected the works to the Glamorgan Canal at Abercynon. In 1804, spectators were treated to the world's first steam locomotive running on a railed track. The experiment was a success in one respect – it worked. At this stage it was simply known as the tram waggon, and Trevithick was delighted.

> The Tram Waggon have been at work several times. It works exceeding well, and is much more manageable than horses. We have not try'd to draw but ten tons at a time yet, but I dought

not but we cou'd draw forty tons at a time very well for ten tons stands no chance at all with it.

There was, however, an ominous sound accompanying the little engine as it puffed its way up and down the tramway; the sound of cracking rails. The brittle cast iron rails were giving way under the weight of the engine. It did continue in use for some time, and Trevithick received another order from a northern colliery, but there too the engine worked but the rails failed. Discouraged by the early results, he decided once again to try and find investors in London. His new locomotive was called *Catch me who can*. He offered to take it to Newmarket where he would back it to beat the best racehorse. However, no one took him up on the offer. So instead, in 1808, he had a circular track built near what is now Euston Square, surrounded by a high wooden fence. He issued adverts promising visitors they would see 'mechanical power subduing animal speed'. They had to pay a shilling for admission, and if they were bold enough, they could take a ride in a truck behind the engine. One of those who took up the offer was John Isaac Hawkins, later to build his own reputation as an engineer. He described the event in an article in the *Mechanics Magazine.*

> He placed a locomotive engine, weighing about 10 tons on that railway, on which I rode, with my watch in hand, at the rate of 12 miles an hour; that Mr. Trevithick then gave his opinion that it would go 20 miles an hour, or more, on a straight railway … it ran for some weeks, when a rail broke and occasioned the engine to fly off in a tangent and overturn, the ground being very soft at the time.

It was yet another London disappointment; the shillings never paid the cost of the scheme, and no one saw the potential for steam railways. The engine was sold off and Trevithick returned to Cornwall, where shortly afterwards he was visited by a gentleman from Peru who wanted him to build high-pressure engines for his silver mine. The engines were sent off, but reports came back that they were not working as well as expected. So, the engineer set off for South America for what he thought would be a short visit. He was away for eleven years. But he still has a part in this story.

The Napoleonic Wars sent the cost of horse feed rocketing, and colliery owners who relied on tramways for transport were

Trevithick's steam locomotive *Catch-me-who-can* was run on a circular track near the site of the present Euston station. It was London's first sight of a railway locomotive but failed to attract any investors.

concerned. John Blenkinsop, who managed the Middleton Colliery just south of Leeds, decided to do something about it. He knew of the earlier experiments and now he bought up Trevithick's patent and commissioned the engineer Matthew Murray of Leeds to design an engine to run on the tramway. But they both knew all about the breaking rails, so they had a problem to solve. A much lighter engine would lack power, but it could do the job if they could increase the traction. The device they came up with was the rack railway. A toothed rail ran down one side of the track, which engaged with a cog on the engine – the system now in use on mountain railways. It was a success, and several mine owners sent their own engineers to see the system. Among them was George Stephenson. He was only one of a number of engineers who set to work building locomotives and his first engine *Blucher* began steaming along the Killingworth colliery tramway in 1814. It was based on the Middleton-Murray engine but without the rack and pinion rail. Unlike the early plateways, the rails were edged rails and the locomotive was fitted with flanged wheels. Significantly, the gauge was 4ft 8in. When Stephenson was engaged to oversee the construction of the far grander Stockton & Darlington Railway, he simply built it to the same gauge – though somewhere at some time an extra half inch crept in. And 4ft 8½in became the standard gauge not just in Britain but on many railways throughout the world.

The Stockton & Darlington was the first public railway to receive an Act that specified that steam locomotives could be used on the line. There is, however, a common misconception about how the line was run. It is true that it carried both freight and passengers, but only freight was moved by steam. Passengers had to make do with a stage coach, pulled by horses that only differed from the normal coaches in having flanged iron wheels so that it could use the tracks. Locomotives trundled along slowly with their loads of coal. The great change came when a decision was taken to build the world's first inter-city railway between Liverpool and Manchester. It was intended to be both a freight and passenger line, but no passengers would want to travel by locomotive if it was slower than the existing stage coaches. Some thought that locomotives were capable of great improvement and could do the job; others

The world's first successful commercial railway was used to carry coal from the Middleton Colliery near Leeds to the River Aire. The train is seen here passing Leeds parish church.

believed that a far better system was to have a series of stationary engines, which would haul trains from one to the other by cable. It was decided to hold a public trial at Rainhill, halfway down the route, in October 1829. Three locomotives competed, but only one met the condition of proving equal to hauling a full train up and down the track, for a distance equal to that between Liverpool and Manchester at an average speed of 10mph. That engine was *Rocket,* designed by Robert Stephenson. It was to be the prototype for a new generation of locomotives that were capable of easily exceeding the modest pace set for the competition. The railway locomotive had come of age, and it was the start of a flurry of rail construction throughout Britain and, inevitably, that included lines in and around London.

The first steam railway for London was proposed in 1825 and, not surprisingly, one of those who opposed the scheme was George Shillibeer, who came up with this merry little rhyme, promoting his horse buses

> These pleasure and comfort with safety combine,
> They will neither blow up nor explode like a mine;
> Those who ride on the railroad might half die with fear,
> You can come to no harm in the safe Shillibeer.

The idea was put forward a little too early to gain public approval, but the London & Greenwich Railway Company was formed in 1831 and received its Act in 1833. The obvious problem was that the route led across a built-up area, and if it had been constructed at street level, would have been either a serious obstacle to road traffic or would have made train travel a nightmare of stops and starts. Instead, it was decided to build it over the streets and houses on a viaduct with 878 brick arches, requiring bricklayers to lay an estimated 60 million bricks.

The first job was to survey the line, and the men had to work their way through the slums of Bermondsey. They were faced with the task of 'laying out the line of road through the most horrible and disgusting part of the metropolis, and during the period when the cholera was raging in that particular neighbourhood'. The canal age had more or less ended, and the workers who had built them, known as navigators, later shortened to navvies, were available to use their strength and expertise for the railway builders. The navvies were divided into two groups and usually

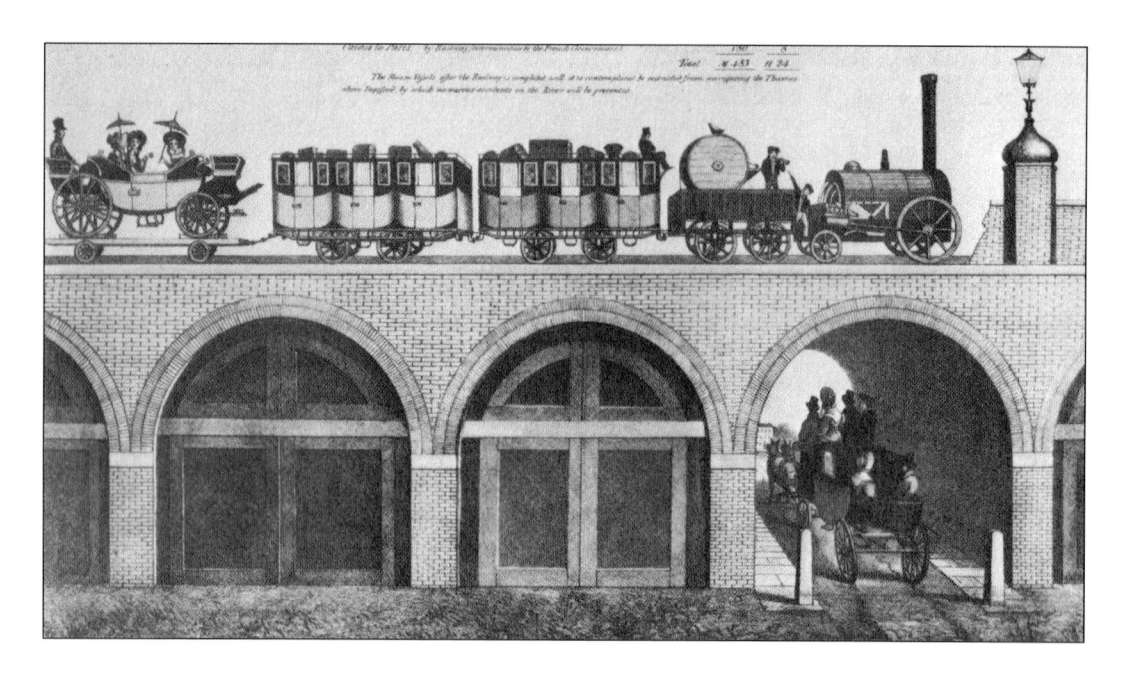

76 • LONDON'S TRANSPORT FROM ROMAN TIMES TO THE PRESENT DAY

London's first steam railway was the London & Greenwich, built over an immense viaduct. Here the train is passing over just two of the 878 arches. Two first class coaches can be seen and trucks were provided for those who wished to travel in their own coaches.

kept themselves to themselves, apart from the times when they got into fights. The two areas became known as English Grounds and Irish Grounds. The track was originally laid, as the tramways were, with rails spiked to stone blocks.

The first locomotives were built by two companies, Charles Tayleur, later to be known as the Vulcan Foundry, based in Newton-le-Willows in Lancashire, and William Marshall of Gravesend. The former provided a 0-2-2 locomotive, shown in the illustration above. For readers unfamiliar with the system, British engines are identified by the numbers of wheels: the first figure refers to wheels supporting the front of the engine, the second to wheels that actually drive it along, and the third figure to wheels supporting the rear end. The Gravesend firm provided three 2-2-2 locomotives. The illustration also shows the engine pulling two first class carriages, which are clearly based on stage coach designs. On the early railways, it was quite usual to have flat trucks to take ladies and gentlemen in their own carriages. Second class were more or less open trucks with seating and a canopy over the top, but open at the sides. Third class were simply trucks which might, or might not, have seats. One company when asked why they didn't supply seats for third class simply replied that you could get more people in if they were standing.

The old coaches, holding only a few passengers, could collect them from an inn, but with trains of carriages there were far more people

THE RAILWAY AGE • 77

to deal with, and a new type of building was required – the railway station. The London terminus was at one end of the great viaduct. Unlike the stations on the pioneering Liverpool & Manchester Railway, London Bridge station was a distinctly spartan affair. They had waiting rooms and platforms with canopies: here there were simply two platforms, approached through elaborate wrought iron gates. It was opened to the public in 1836 and four years later a tarred canvas roof was added to offer some protection. This did not seem to deter travellers for on the Whit Monday following the opening, 13,000 passengers travelled the line. The line was a success, but over time as more lines were constructed, congestion became a major problem.

First on the scene was the London & Croydon Railway (L&CR) who used part of the same track but had to buy some of the land owned by the original company to construct their own station. They were then joined by the London & Brighton Railway (L&BR). They were shortly afterwards joined by the South Eastern Railway

The original station at London Bridge that served the London & Greenwich and eventually several other lines. At first, the facilities for passengers were almost non-existent.

(SER). Now things became really complicated. The old L&CR station was hopelessly inadequate, and plans were drawn up for a new station to be built in an elaborate Italianate style, complete with a campanile, though it is not clear whether any bells were ever going to be hung on it. However, everyone agreed it would be highly decorative. It was opened as a station in 1844, before all the buildings were completed. But now, the L&CR and the L&BR had become decidedly aggrieved by the high charges being made for use of the L&GR tracks and decided to build their own London Bridge station. This left the Greenwich Company desperately short of funds and the SER took over their station. The London & Brighton merged with the old Croydon Railway to form the London, Brighton & South Coast Railway (LB&SCR), so now there were two quite independent lines, next to each other, Eventually there was a joint station, with a dividing wall, with the SER on one side and the LB&SCR on the other. The two sides were only finally united in 1923. There were more changes that continued right through to the present day, but one can reasonably say that, readers will no doubt be relieved to hear, no other station ever had quite such a convoluted history.

The London & South Western Railway began life as the London & Southampton, when it received its Act in 1834, but was renamed when it was extended to Plymouth. Originally, the London end of the line was at Nine Elms, but a great deal of the traffic was quite local, made up of commuters coming in from areas such as Wimbledon and Wandsworth. It seemed sensible to extend the line closer to the city centre and a new station was built close to the southern edge of Waterloo Bridge. It carried four tracks and the approach was, rather like the L&GR, largely on a series of brick arches to carry it above the existing roads. One result of this was that the approach for passengers was up a ramp. It was never really intended as a terminus, so as traffic increased, the company simply stuck an extra piece on the side. One of these extras was unique, in that many of the passengers it took were dead. It was built for the London Necropolis and National Mausoleum Company and ran to their Brookwood Cemetery, said to be the largest in Europe. I first became aware that such a line had once existed not from reading railway history but from a thriller by Andrew Martin, *The Necropolis Railway* published in 2003. The original Waterloo station was finally reconstructed at the start of the twentieth century.

Coaches outside the old Waterloo station.

An illustration from the *Practical Mechanics' Magazine* of 1848 showing the latest in locomotive technology, the locomotive built for the London, Brighton & South Coast Railway that year.

In the same year as the L&GR received its authorizing Act, another far grander scheme received official approval – the London & Birmingham Railway. The engineer in charge was Robert Stephenson and he faced the problems common to all working on long transport links – coping with the terrain by embankments and bridges, cuttings and tunnels. But he also faced the difficulty of bringing the line in through a heavily built-up area of North London, Camden Town. But where the engineer of the London & Greenwich had sailed high above the houses, Stephenson charged right through the middle of them in a deep cutting. The resulting chaos for the citizens was vividly described by Charles Dickens in his novel, *Dombey and Son*.

> Houses were knocked down, streets broken through and stopped, deep pits and trenches dug in the ground; enormous heaps of earth and clay thrown up: buildings that were undermined and shaking, propped by great beams of wood. Here, a chaos of carts, overthrown and jumbled together, lay topsy-turvy at the bottom of a steep, unnatural hill; there confused treasures of iron soaked and rusted in something that had accidentally become a pond. Everywhere there were bridges that led nowhere, thoroughfares that were wholly impassable; babel towers of chimneys, wanting half their height; temporary wooden houses and enclosures in the most unlikely situations; carcases of ragged tenements, and fragments of unfinished walls and arches, and piles of scaffolding, and wildernesses of brick, and giant forms of cranes, and tripods straddling above nothing.

A drawing by J.C. Bourne of 1839, showing workers on the London & Birmingham Railway where it was slicing through Camden Town in a deep cutting.

There was, however, a limit beyond which no railway could be allowed to advance. Stephenson had hoped to take the lines all the way to Marble Arch, but that was turned down and a second suggestion was made to end at Maiden Lane, not the street near Covent Garden, but the road now known as York Way. It also received a thumbs down from the authorities. So, everything came to a halt at what would become the London terminus, Euston Station. There was a problem with the site, in that the line had to climb steeply from Camden Town to cross the Regent's Canal and the engines of the day were not up to the task. As a result, a stationary steam engine had to be placed at the top of the slope to haul trains up by cable. This first station was comparatively simple, consisting of just two platforms, one for arrivals and one for departures, with a pitched glass roof carried on elegant iron colonnades. The entrance to the station, however, was far more impressive, a grand classical arch, designed by the station's architect, Philip Hardwick. Either side of the arch were two hotels, the forerunners of railway hotels that would be a feature of towns and cities throughout the land.

The old Euston station in an aquatint by T.T. Bury. It is notable that there is just one first class carriage in view, but the third class open carriages are abundant and crowded.

The splendid Euston arch that made an imposing entrance to the station, photographed in the 1890s. It was demolished in a modernization programme of the 1960s.

The railway proved far more successful than the promoters had ever dreamed possible, and by 1849 a major extension programme was put in hand, which included the construction of the Great Hall, which was indeed great. But the Great Hall and the Euston Arch both fell victim to the modernisation that took place starting in 1959. It was inevitable that the Hall had to go, but there still seems to be no good reason for losing the Arch. There was a public protest led by Sir John Betjeman, but to no avail. The new station, still being subject to change, has lost all its former glamour.

Not long after work started on the London & Birmingham Railway, another railway venture was begun in the west of England, and the Great Western Railway was formally approved in 1838, with the young Isambard Kingdom Brunel as its Chief Engineer. He had travelled on the Liverpool & Manchester and had not been impressed by the comfort of the ride. He was convinced that the problem was largely down to the fact that the track was too narrow: trains could get a smoother, faster ride on a wider track. His railway would not make do with a niggardly 4ft 8½in track but would have rails set 7ft apart. It would be a broad gauge railway. Not only would it be wider but it would be constructed in a quite different way. We see sleepers under the rails, being set at intervals at right angles to the track. Brunel's rails would be set on longitudinal wooden sleepers running the full length of the rails, and held in a rigid framework by cross ties. To Brunel's credit, he had thought seriously about what would make for the best track design, unlike George Stephenson, who had blithely copied the gauge of the old colliery lines. Ultimately, whatever advantages the Brunel system may have had there was no avoiding the fact that most of the country had followed the Stephenson example, and ultimately the broad gauge was doomed. But Londoners were soon to have two routes – they could travel to Birmingham and the north on one system and to Bristol and the west on another.

The original idea was to join the London & Birmingham at Euston, but when that plan fell through, a new site for a terminus was chosen on the outskirts of west London at Paddington. At least Brunel had a much easier approach route, as all he needed to do was follow the line of the Paddington branch of the Grand Junction Canal. The first station, however, was a very modest affair, built to the west of the present station. Like Euston it soon proved hopelessly inadequate. Brunel designed the new station in 1853 and it is one of the glories of the rail network. It has been called the cathedral of the steam age, and there is something decidedly

The first rather primitive Paddington station was built slightly to the west of the present station.

ecclesiastical about the design. The huge glass roof has three spans, like the nave and side aisles, and they were originally joined by two transepts. The ornate cast iron pillars were designed by the architect Matthew Digby Wyatt, who also provided the slightly Moorish looking window to the offices. Although more platforms have been added over the years, and other alterations have been made, the original train shed remains much as it was. Unlike Euston, there is no grand entrance. The whole station is set in a cutting and the main pedestrian entrance from Praed Street could hardly be less imposing, no more than a ramp leading down to platform level. That simply makes what one sees on arriving at the bottom seem all the more wonderful. I am, perhaps, somewhat prejudiced, as Paddington has been my gateway to London from my home in the west of England for the last forty odd years and I still get a thrill from looking at the sublime blend of engineering skill and architectural finesse. There is now a statue of Brunel near the entrance, but he would perhaps not have expected to share the honour with a duffel-coated bear.

Londoners now had rail access to the west and the northwest of England and lines were also being extended up into Scotland, so the next stage was more or less inevitable – a main line to the northeast. Not everyone, however, welcomed the move. The London &

Brunel's Paddington station as it appeared in the nineteenth century.

Birmingham were enjoying a profitable monopoly of train services to the north, and other smaller companies feared a new line would cost them as well. The battle to get an Act through parliament was bitterly fought and at huge expense for all involved, but eventually the Great Northern received permission for a route to link London to York and on up to Edinburgh. It was by far the biggest scheme yet proposed, with a total of 327 miles of railway, that included the main line and branches. The first temporary station was at Maiden Lane, where Robert Stephenson had originally proposed to end his line. It was later moved to its present site and opened as King's Cross in 1852. It is the perfect example of what is often referred to as engineers' architecture – a phrase I first came across in an article by Sir John Betjeman. One can see exactly what it means before you

Paddington today. The 'transept' adds to the cathedral-like quality of the great iron and glass roof.

even enter the station itself. The frontage is plain but dramatic – two great brick arches with a tall campanile in the centre. The arches tell you what you'll find inside, a great double arched glass roof, originally covering the departure platform to one side, arrivals the other, magnificent in its bold simplicity. It was mainly the work of a man whose name has largely been forgotten, Lewis Cubitt, brother of the more famous Thomas Cubitt. Like all London's biggest stations, it has grown over the years and for a time in the latter part of the twentieth century, the façade was marred by an ungainly, boring extension. Thankfully, the excrescence was removed in 2007 and the original façade and train shed restored. In the process the old station also acquired a new elegant concourse. It was once considered rather inferior to Euston, but no more.

The Midland Railway was created by the 'Railway King' George Hudson, from an amalgamation of smaller lines, all centred on Derby. One thing it lacked was its own station in London. The lines steadily extended southwards and by 1858 had reached the Great Northern at Hitchin, and from there they paid to use the latter's lines into King's Cross. It was never a happy arrangement. Not surprisingly, the Midland trains were always at the bottom of the list when it came to priorities. Delays built up, and eventually the

King's Cross station. The facade echoes the two curved roofs over the arrival and departure platforms.

Midland decided to build their own route to London from Bedford. The company's main traffic was in coal from the Midland and northern coalfields, so the first stage was to construct a large goods depot, between 1862 and 1865. But it was also decided that they needed a passenger station, as much for prestige as profit, and they purchased an area of land on the Euston Road from Lord Somers, and promptly began knocking down seven streets of houses and evicting an estimated 10,000 tenants.

The station takes its name from a nearby church dedicated to the early Christian martyr, Saint Pancras of Rome. For most people, the image that comes to mind when thinking of the station is not the actual station at all, but the flamboyant Midland Hotel at the front. We'll come on to that shortly, but first there is the extraordinary station itself, the work of the engineer, William Henry Barlow. His design was absolutely astonishing for the time. The train shed was to be covered by one giant glazed arch, with a span of 245ft 6in, at the time and for decades to come the largest of its kind in the world. The whole is supported by 24 wrought iron ribs. The outward thrust of the arch is restrained by iron girders, hidden away beneath the tracks. Down in the undercroft, the space is arranged to take an important part of the Midland's trade – bringing in hogsheads of beer from Burton-on-Trent. Everything about it is practical, but it has its own grandeur.

Contractors posing in front of the vaults below St. Pancras station that were specially designed to take hogsheads of beer from Burton-on-Trent.

The vast roof of St. Pancras under construction.

The hotel was completed the year after the station opened, designed by Sir Gilbert Scott, in what was then the very latest style, full-on Gothic. If architecturally it looked to the past, inside it was the epitome of modernity, the first to have electric bells to summon staff, and hydraulically operated lifts. The interior was as grand as the exterior, dominated by the grand staircase. Victorian architecture fell out of fashion in the twentieth century and as a result, the hotel, once the grandest in London, became neglected and turned into shabby offices, but tastes have changed, and it has now been gloriously restored. If you want to see the two faces of Victorian buildings, the works of architects and engineers, then there are few better places to come than St. Pancras. Like all London main line stations, there have been changes over the years, but the most dramatic happened here, when it was chosen as the terminus for Eurostar, the service through the Channel Tunnel linking Britain to mainland Europe, that began in 2007. There was a happy acknowledgement, however, to one of St. Pancras's most enthusiastic advocates, when a statue of Sir John Betjeman was installed which, unlike many statues in public places, is full of life and catches something of his effervescent personality.

While major new stations were being built at Paddington and up and down the Euston Road, a more modest building appeared, within the boundaries of the city for the first time. The City authorities had finally relented and allowed tracks to penetrate the hallowed spaces of the old city. In fact, it reached the very heart of the city, for right next to the station are some of the remains of the old Roman wall. It was built for a very modest company, the London & Blackwall Extension Railway. When the railway first opened, it ran from a temporary station at Minories, which was then replaced by Fenchurch Street. It was an odd line, originally planned by John Rennie, but actually built under the supervision of Robert Stephenson. He inherited Rennie's scheme, which involved track at the strange gauge of 5ft ½in. He then decided, because of the gradients involved, to use cable haulage by steam engine, as he had at Camden Town. The line served London's dockland and no one felt the need for a very grand station and, apart from an Italianate frontage, is functional rather than dramatic. The line was later taken over by the Eastern Counties Railway, who ran the line with steam locomotives and changed the track to standard gauge.

A statue of the great enthusiast for Victorian railway architecture, Sir John Betjeman, at St. Pancras.

They also extended the route to Southend, which became the favourite seaside resort for generations of East Enders.

If the original London & Blackwall line was unusual, it was nowhere near as strange as the London & Croydon. The complex situation with the original London & Croydon, sharing facilities at London Bridge with the London & Greenwich and later the London & Brighton, had led to a great many problems, particularly with slow local trains holding up the main line services. William Cubitt suggested a solution – build a third track beside the original two that would be used by local trains in both directions, freeing up the main line. So far, so sensible but then a new idea was put forward. In 1841, Joseph Samuda wrote a treatise promoting the idea of an atmospheric railway. There would be a conventional track, but between the rails was an iron pipe with a slit in the top, running the whole length of the route. Inside the pipe was a piston and at the

The cable-haulage system that was used to overcome the steep gradients on the London & Blackwall Extension Railway.

end of the track was a steam engine. The leading vehicle of the train was connected through the slit to a flange on the piston. The whole of the rest of the slit was covered by a metal reinforced leather strip. The engine pumped air out of the pipe, creating a partial vacuum in front of the piston – and air pressure from the other end forced the piston down the pipe, taking the train on the tracks above with it. This was the system that was installed on the London & Croydon and the first section opened in 1844. Initial trials were a great success. A train of ten carriages set off smoothly from Dartmouth Arms to a top speed of 54mph, and reached Croydon five miles away in just under 9 minutes. The trouble with such systems is that they rely on stationary engines. If a steam locomotive breaks down, it can be shunted out of the way and replaced quite quickly. If one of the big steam engines breaks, nothing can be done until it is repaired. And that, sadly, is what happened on the London & Croydon more than once. By 1847, the system was abandoned. The little line would have been no more than an anomaly in the story of London's transport, but the atmospheric system won over one of the greatest engineers of the day, Isambard Brunel. He famously installed it on his new line linking Exeter to Plymouth. It too was short lived and must be counted as perhaps his greatest engineering failure.

The first station from which tracks headed south from a site on the north bank of the Thames was Charing Cross, built for the London, Chatham & Dover Railway (LC&DR). It says perhaps all one needs to know about the qualities of the station buildings that

The London & Croydon atmospheric railway, in which the trains are attached to a piston moving down the tube between the rails. The arches of the London & Greenwich Railway can be seen in the distance.

it is one of the few London termini not to make it onto the pages of Simon Jenkins' 2017 book, *Britain's Hundred Best Railway Stations*. It is, however, of interest for at least two reasons. After its opening in 1864, it became one of the places from which one could catch a boat train to be whisked off to Europe. Secondly, the bridge across the Thames had a pedestrian path beside the tracks, making the old Hungerford suspension bridge redundant. It was demolished, but the chains found a new home, being used to complete the Clifton suspension bridge, begun by Isambard Brunel. Rather like St. Pancras, the most obvious striking feature when approaching the station is the railway hotel at the front, in the French renaissance style, perhaps rather appropriate for guests staying over to take a holiday in Paris.

The station had to be completely rebuilt following an accident on 5 December 1905 just before 4 o'clock in the afternoon. Men were working on glazing and painting the roof, when they heard an ominous crack, and saw one of the tie rods had broken. The roof began to sag and the western wall started to crack. There was a rush to get people off trains and out of the station and to halt incoming trains, but there was just a twelve-minute gap between the first sign of trouble before the roof fell in and the wall collapsed. Six people died in the accident and all the tracks were blocked by debris. It was decided not to replace the original curved roof, but instead put on a far simpler, ridge and furrow roof. The station partially reopened in 1906.

In 1861, the LC&DR decided there would be a great advantage in extending their system eastwards to the City of London and received permission to construct Cannon Street Station. The design was functional, with a single arched train shed, with two towers on either side, looking out to the Thames. The new development also included building a bridge over the Thames to provide a connection to London Bridge. Over the years, the station has gone through numerous transformations. The service between Charing Cross and Cannon Street was unable to compete once the London Underground arrived but the suburban services remained valuable. The second half of the twentieth century saw the original train shed demolished along with the railway hotel, and an office block built over the station in the 1950s, and that in its turn was replaced by an altogether more elegant new mixed use building, which made Cannon Street the only main line station to have a roof garden. Of the original station all that remains are the two towers, which now have listed building status, so they at least should remain unchanged.

THE RAILWAY AGE • 93

A train about to emerge from Cannon Street station in a drawing of 1923, while a Thames barge and a rowed lighter pass by on the river.

Cannon Street station today, complete with roof garden and office development.

Victoria Station has, like so many London stations, had a complex history. The Crystal Palace built for the Great Exhibition of 1851 was hugely popular, but its home in Hyde Park was always to be temporary. So, it was taken apart and rebuilt in Sydenham, where it continued to draw the crowds. The London Bridge & South Coast Railway (LB&SCR) opened a branch line to Sydenham, while at the same time a new company, the West End of London & Crystal Palace Railway (WL&CPR), began building a line to a new station at Battersea. It was a very temporary affair and part of the new line was rapidly leased by the LB&SCR. They realized that the line would be far more useful if it had a new terminus across the river. They had competition, however, as there were other companies interested in building on the site – the Great Western, the London & North Western and the East Kent. As a result, these three railways and the WL&CPR amalgamated to form the Victoria Station & Pimlico Railway. The LB&SCR had hoped to join the consortium, but instead had to make do with their own station, while the consortium had their terminus alongside. For a long time, Victoria had a Chatham side and a Brighton side. The Chatham side was also to be the one that served the port of Dover and had the catchy slogan 'Gateway to the Continent'. The Brighton line was less exotic but served England's most fashionable resort. When in *The Importance of Being Earnest* Jack Worthing disclosed that he had been found, rather ignominiously, in a handbag, he was at least able to claim the distinction that it was on the Brighton line, but famously that failed to impress Lady Bracknell. The stations were given new facades in the early twentieth century in the then fashionable Baroque style, but it was not until railways were split into larger groups in 1923 and both the competing companies were amalgamated to form the Southern Railway that the dividing wall was demolished and the two Victoria Stations became one.

An essential part of the whole development of Victoria Station was the construction of a new bridge across the Thames, Grosvenor Bridge, named after the Grosvenor estate on which the station had been built. The original was built by the Victoria & Pimlico and completed in 1860 to take two tracks, later widened to four tracks in 1865 and another track added in 1907. The whole structure was completely rebuilt in the 1960s, crossing the river in four elegant, low arches.

The Great Eastern Railway was formed in 1862 from an amalgamation of four companies serving the east of England.

Liverpool Street station still retains its Victorian splendour.

Originally, the terminus was the modest Bishopsgate station, which had served the Norwich and King's Lynn line, but which soon proved to be hopelessly inadequate to cope with the increase in traffic. The company not only needed a bigger station, but also one nearer the centre of the city. The eventual site chosen was to become home to the Liverpool Street station. It was to be built in a heavily populated area of London, so armed with a compulsory purchase order, the company bought up a large swathe of land for the station and the approach tracks, resulting in some 10,000 people being evicted. The result was one of London's great stations, with a magnificent train shed, with four spans of wrought iron based on ornate cast iron columns. Few stations have a grander entrance, flanked by two towers that promise something special when one goes inside. And that is just what one finds, with a double staircase leading down to the main concourse. All this was threatened when

British Rail in its enthusiasm for modernization proposed pulling it all down and replacing it by a new terminus, just as it had at Euston and with results that were likely to prove equally drab. But there was a huge public outcry, and instead of demolition, the station was rebuilt but most of the original features were preserved.

The last main line station to be built in London had its origins in the north of England, where the Manchester, Sheffield & Lincolnshire Railway was struggling to make a profit, and the solution seemed to be to create a line down to the capital, which would become the Great Central Railway. Providing the last section of the line down to London proved troublesome, and one obstacle to progress was the proposed line to be taken. As originally planned, it would have been built over Lord's cricket ground, which was, of course, unthinkable. For cricket lovers it was tantamount to a proposal to running tracks through the heart of Westminster Abbey. Once it was clear that Lord's would remain untouched, work could go ahead for a new station just off the Marylebone Road. The company had never had much cash to spare, so the design was left to the company's engineer H.W. Braddock, with instructions to keep everything simple, with no unnecessary flourishes. No self-respecting main line station could do without a station hotel, but the Great Central could only manage the station, so the contract for the hotel went to Sir Blundell Maple, owner of the highly successful furniture company of Maple's. If the station was plain, the hotel was extravagant, built in the Neo-Jacobean style. The station opened to passengers in 1899 and the hotel was ready to greet them. It was a vast affair of 700 rooms, but like the railway itself never really prospered. For a while it was turned into offices and became British Rail headquarters. Today, it has been restored to its former glory as the Landmark Hotel.

The stations discussed so far have all been main line terminals, taking passengers and freight out of London to various parts of the country. There was also a growing network providing purely local services. The first to be developed were mainly short lines serving the London docks north of the river, one of which, the London & Blackwall Railway, was extended to Islington in 1850 to become the North London Railway. It was then developed as a joint venture with the London and North Western Railway to Richmond. Then, in 1865, the companies acquired a proper terminus at Broad Street, next to Liverpool Street Station. It was never very grand, but the line was useful in its day, though use declined with the development of other forms of London transport, especially the Underground. When I first started work in London, I was living in North London and this was the line I took each day to a laboratory in Chiswick. The rolling stock was showing its age, the journey was carried out at what might be termed a modest pace. But when I left there for a job in central London, I missed the calm of the old line as I joined everyone else crammed into tube trains. Broad Street, however, failed to survive. It closed for good in 1986.

So far, we have simply been concentrating on the construction of the lines in and around London, but in the next chapter we shall be looking at what it was like to travel on them in the age of the steam train.

A railway map of 1899 showing the network at that time with the overground railways shown as solid lines.

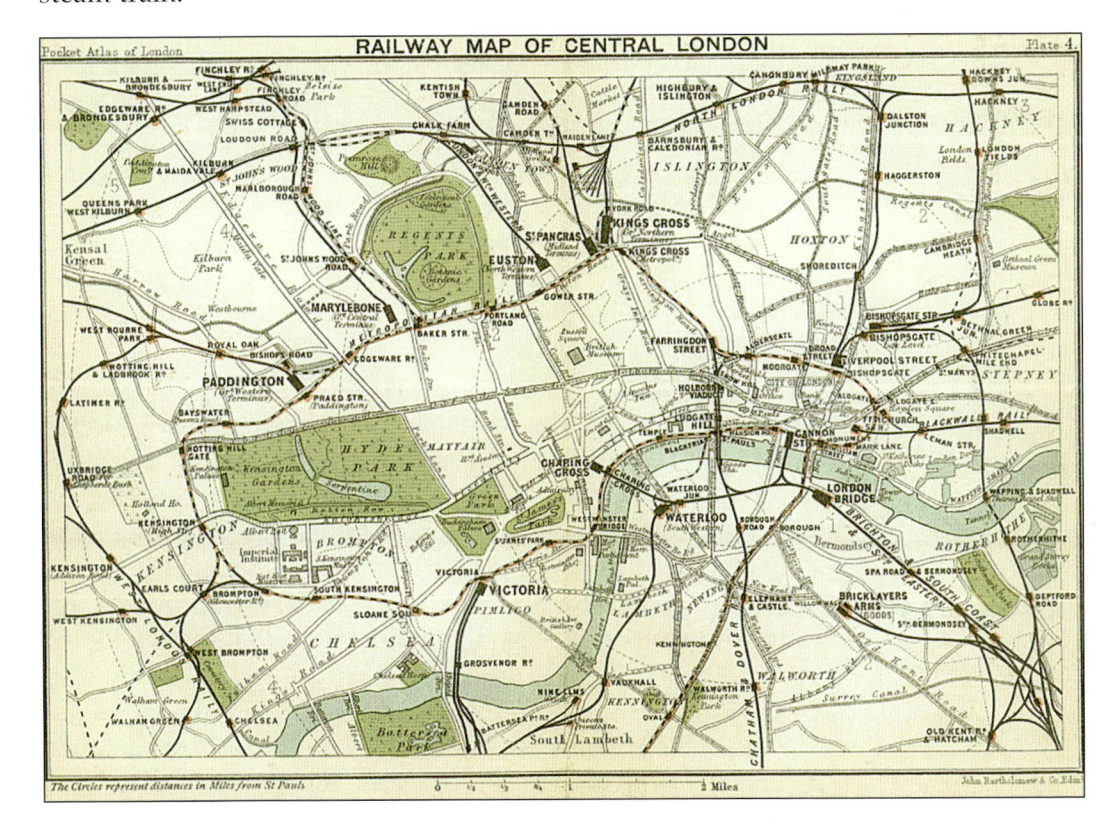

CHAPTER FIVE

Train Travel in the Steam Age

Rail travel became popular from the day when the very first railway was opened in London, but whether it was a pleasant experience or something to be patiently endured depended on several factors: journey speed and reliability, comfort and safety being the most important. Speed and reliability depended to a large extent on the skill of the engineers who designed the engines and the companies who manufactured them. One London company which built their own engines was the London & South Western who established their works at Nine Elms in 1839, only for them to be almost totally destroyed by a fire in 1841. A new works was opened on the same site two years later, but as the system expanded, so the old works was unable to cope. However, in the twenty years they were in operation, over 100 locomotives were built designed by Joseph Hamilton Beattie and John Viret Gooch, the brother of the famous Daniel Gooch, chief engineer for the Great Western. In the 1860s, work was transferred to a larger site nearby. It remained in use right through to the start of the twentieth century, when once again the work outgrew the site and everything was moved to Eastleigh in Hampshire. For much of its history, the Nine Elms works relied on the Beattie family, Joseph being joined by his son William. Joseph was an innovative engineer. All early locomotives were fired using coke to avoid pollution from smoke fumes. It was, however, less efficient and more expensive than coal and Beattie was among the first to design locomotives designed for coal firing. It was certainly successful in purely engineering terms, but coal fired engines did exactly what their detractors had feared, adding hugely to pollution, especially in towns and cities. Most early locomotives had just four wheels, and Beattie was among the first to introduce a new type of engine, with two pairs of drive wheels coupled together – the 2-4-0s. One of his most successful models was a 2-4-0 well tank, the tank holding water for the boiler. His 0298 class were extraordinarily successful. The first of the class model rolled out of Nine Elms in 1874 and the last was only retired from service in 1962, but even in retirement examples can still be found running on preserved lines.

A preserved 2-4-0 locomotive designed by Joseph Beattie for the London & South Western Railway seen here at the Buckinghamshire Rail Centre at Quainton. It has been modified over the years, most notably by the addition of a closed cab for the crew.

Speed on the line increased steadily and by 1899, the L&SWR had introduced its T-9 class of 4-4-0 locomotives, better known as the 'Greyhound' class. On one notable occasion, one of these locomotives brought the Plymouth boat express from Templecombe to Waterloo, covering the 112½ miles at an average speed of 65mph. The best service on offer today for a journey from Waterloo to Plymouth has an average speed of 46mph. Such is progress.

The North London Railway had a site at Bow, originally simply used for repairing locomotives, but by 1860 it had been enlarged so that locomotives could also be built there. One of the features of the line was the sharpness of some of the curves and the locomotive superintendent, William Adams, invented a special form of sliding bogie for the four front wheels on his 4-4-0 tank engines. This type of tank engine continued to be built right up to 1906, when the works closed. For nearly half a century it had supplied reliable, if not desperately exciting, engines for this suburban service.

The 'Greyhound' locomotives designed by the engineer Dugald Drummond for the L&SWR were the latest thing in express travel when they first appeared on the tracks in 1899.

Most of the main lines had their own engineering works outside London, in important railway centres such as Swindon, Crewe and Derby. One manufacturer in the London area, however, has a special place in railway history. George England set up works at New Cross in Lewisham in 1839, supplying a variety of engines for various companies, including the London & Blackwall and the London, Brighton & South Coast, but his main achievement had nothing to do with London lines, but instead was concerned with what had originally been a tramway serving the slate mines of North Wales. The Ffestiniog Railway opened in 1836. The line ran from Blaenau Ffestiniog to a new port at Port Madoc, now Porthmadog. It was steep and full of tight bends, and because all the main loads were being taken downhill, the trucks went down under gravity and the empties were pulled back up by horses. It was always going to be an isolated line so when it came to gauge, it was simply built to fit in with the tracks already in use at the quarry at just 23½ inches. When Charles Spooner took over the running of the railway, he decided in 1862 to abandon the horses and turn to steam locomotives, and the company he chose to construct the engines was George England. They were the first successful locomotives ever to be built for a narrow-gauge line. The first two delivered were named *Princess* and *Mountaineer*. The Princess was soon to get her *Prince*, and the little 0-4-0 tank engines did the job well. But two years later, the line was authorized to carry passengers as well as freight. This was a single-track line, and there was never any possibility of doubling up a line that was already 'it seemed' clinging precariously to the hillside. The only way to cope with the extra traffic was to have longer trains, but this proved too much of a strain for the old engines. The answer to the problem of building a powerful engine that could still cope with the tight bends was provided by Robert Fairlie. Nothing like them had ever been seen before, a sort of push-me-pull-yous looking like two locomotives that had been stuck together back-to-back. There was a central cab, between two boilers. The secret to their success lay in the use of two swivelling bogies, one for each end. In action, the engines provided a strange sight when going round a steep curve, with one set of wheels pointing one way and the other in a different direction. They too were made by John England, but shortly afterwards the name of the company was changed to Fairlie Engine and Steam Carriage Company. It was destined to be short lived, closing down in 1869. The early England engines, however, have survived and many are still running after a century and a half of use. There are no locomotives anywhere in the world that have such a history of continuous service on the line for which they were built.

There was a steady improvement in speed and performance of locomotives. Often this was a matter of company pride, but in other cases something of a necessity. Londoners wanting to travel to Scotland had a choice of routes: up the east coast from King's Cross

The George
England-built locomotive *Prince* at Porthmadog on the Ffestiniog Railway was built in 1863. This was only the third locomotive to be built for any narrow gauge line.

A double-ended Fairlie locomotive on the Ffestiniog Railway in its working days with a long train of slate wagons. The engine was specially designed to cope with tight curves.

or the west coast from Euston. The competing companies vied to make the fastest runs in what came to be known as the 'races to the north'. The fastest runs to Aberdeen were made on 22 August 1895, with the 540 miles from Euston being covered in 8 hours 32 minutes at an average speed of 63.3mph, just pipping the King's Cross route where the 523½ miles took 8 hours 38 minutes at an average of 62.3mph. It could best be described as an honourable draw. The fastest section on the Euston run was between Crewe and Carlisle with an average of 67.2mph, and as this included the climb over the notoriously steep Shap Fell it was a remarkable achievement and a tribute to the locomotive *Hardwicke*, now preserved in the National Railway Museum at York, and its driver B. Robinson.

Passenger comfort, particularly for the cheaper classes, was notably slower to develop. For a long time, third class passengers were still being carried in open trucks, with the greatest indignity reserved for anyone booking a third class ticket on the Great Western. They found themselves linked, not to one of the latest expresses, but attached to a slow goods train. The companies were unwilling to change and it took a major accident for change to be forced on them. On Christmas Eve 1842 at 4.30 in the morning, a goods train left London with two open third class coaches attached. Heavy rainfall had led to a landslide in the deep Sonning cutting and in the darkness the train ploughed straight into it. The goods wagons were loosely coupled and the impact sent them crashing forward, crushing the passenger compartments into the back of the tender. Eight men were killed and seventeen seriously injured. It was not just the seriousness of the accident that roused parliament to take action, but the men had all been working on the new House of Commons and were on their way home for Christmas. A Board of Trade enquiry was set up and as a result, a law was passed ordering all railway companies to provide at least one train a day in each direction, with third class carriages with both seats and overhead covers that had to travel at a speed of not less than 12mph at a fare of a penny a mile.

The Act had a knock-on effect. If third class passengers were getting coaches more or less identical to those of the second class, why should anyone pay more for the same level of comfort? Companies were forced to improve the second class, by introducing such luxuries as padded seats. Eastern Counties coaches had first and second in the same vehicle. The centre portion was wide, with windows in the top of the door and to either side and upholstered seating with headrests. The two second class at either

Hardwicke **was** one of the locomotives that took part in the record breaking 'races to the north'. The locomotive is now preserved at the National Railway Museum in York.

A busy scene at Bishopsgate Station on the Eastern Counties Railway.

end, were narrower with just the one window in the door, and less comfortable seats with no headrests. The coaches themselves were still very basic, carried on two pairs of spoked wheels and had no built-in lighting. Anyone travelling by night could hire an oil lamp that could be hung on a hook in the carriage. Over the years the system was improved, and gas lighting was first introduced for trains in 1863. The best system was the Pintsch oil-gas system, in which liquified gas was kept in cylinders under each coach and piped up to the carriages. In 1875, the Midland finally abolished second class altogether, and most other companies eventually followed their lead.

The first coaches were always quite low – anyone over six foot would be unlikely to be able to stand up straight. There were no corridors and therefore no lavatories. Desperate passengers would have to decide whether they could hold out a bit longer or make a dash for the station loo and hope to be back before the train set off again. The one exception was the Great Western, where there was a twenty-minute compulsory stop at Swindon. The first British coach with a lavatory was built in 1860. Heating was non-existent on most trains until the twentieth century. Dining facilities on trains were only introduced in the 1870s. However, passengers were prepared to put up with the discomfort for the undoubted advantages of travelling by train, and not just available to those with large incomes. An important part of the work of the London

TRAIN TRAVEL IN THE STEAM AGE • **105**

The luxury of first class travel in the nineteenth century in a painting of 1854 by Abraham Solomon.

In contrast to the previous picture, this one shows life in the third class. It is ironically called 'Seats for five persons'.

An illustration from *The Engineer* of a gas lit carriage: the gas cylinder is beneath the carriage and is then piped up to the compartments.

lines was running excursion trains, whether to the seaside or for special events such as the Epsom Derby.

By the latter part of the nineteenth century, new standards were developed. Coaches with six or eight wheels came into use with corridors, linking compartments and coaches. But one big change came from America. George Mortimer Pullman had plans for improving the rolling stock with a new variety of heavy, luxury coach, but none of the big railway companies were interested, so he set up in business on his own. The first coach was timber on an iron frame, carried on two four-wheeled bogies, with springs and rubber shock absorbers. Passengers enjoyed the luxury of individual chairs that could be converted into beds, and there were tables between the chairs, so that passengers could be served meals without making a special journey to a restaurant car. Everything about the coaches was luxurious from the thick pile carpet to the wood panelling. In spite of that, they were not an immediate success, but Pullman achieved a brilliant PR coup. When Abraham Lincoln was assassinated, he offered a Pullman car to take the body from Washington back to his hometown in Illinois.

Pullman coaches were soon being introduced into Britain. They were always considered very special, and there was generally a premium to be paid for taking the Pullman rather than an ordinary train. The through coach was very unusual and caused me an embarrassment, when many years ago I took a job as a temporary porter during the University vacation. I was asked by an elderly lady

The Derby at Epsom was a huge attraction, and this picture shows setting off in first, second and third class.

to help her put her luggage on the rack. With a normal compartment that was never a problem, but her seat was right in the middle and by the time I'd got down there and was making my way back, the train had started. I spent most of that day travelling for over an hour to the first stop and then waiting for a train to get me back again.

The twentieth century saw huge improvements in passenger comfort, with heating in winter, electric lighting and dining cars. There was also a move by several companies to follow the Pullman practice of introducing special luxury trains. One of these was the Coronation, named after the coronation of George VI, that made its first run for the London & North Eastern in July 1937, leaving King's Cross at 4 p.m. and arriving in Edinburgh just six hours later. Everything about it looked modern. The train was usually headed by a streamlined A4 Pacific locomotive, made famous when one of the class *'Mallard'* set a new world speed record of 126mph – a record that it still holds for steam locomotives. The carriages were equally modern, in the fashionable art deco style, and included an observation car in summer. Passenger comfort had come a long way in the century that had passed since the first steam train puffed slowly away from London Bridge.

Another factor that was fundamental to the success of rail travel was safety. Famously, the first person to be run over and killed was the MP William Huskisson at the opening of the Liverpool & Manchester Railway. No one at that time had got used to the speed of trains, and he had wandered over the tracks to talk to the Duke of Wellington, just as *Rocket* with George Stephenson driving came thundering towards him. He seemed as confused as a rabbit in a

The London & North Eastern Railway Coronation expresses were the latest thing in modern deluxe travel in the 1930s. This postcard, one of a set of three, shows the observation car at the rear of the train.

TRAIN TRAVEL IN THE STEAM AGE • **109**

"THE CORONATION"

The art deco styling of a first class carriage on the Coronation express.

"THE CORONATION"

Third class on the Coronation was not as grand as first, but still offered a level of comfort that was exceptional for the time.

car's headlights – the locomotive ran over his legs and although he was rushed to hospital, he died the same day. The accident might have been avoided had there been any indication that the locomotive was approaching, but it was another accident of a quite different kind in 1833 that led to an answer to that problem. A train hit a cart loaded with eggs and milk, and though no one was hurt, there was the makings of a very large omelette spread across the tracks. George Stephenson went to see a musical instrument maker in Leicester, and together they came up with what they called a steam trumpet – later known as the steam whistle, which became a standard fitting.

A far more pressing problem was how to avoid locomotives colliding. The first system was simply to have a ten-minute time gap between trains using the same track. This was all very well, but it made no allowance for one train being faster than the other, or for unexpected delays. Railway policemen were positioned at various points along the track to offer some sort of control by means of hand signals: arms at the side for road clear; arm held out to the side for stop; and arms held up at 45° for slow down. There was still a problem – such signals were useless at night. The first crude night signalling system consisted of lanterns hung on a tall post: a white light for the all clear, red for stop. When a train went by, the signalman went up the ladder and replaced the white light with the red. He then waited the required ten minutes and then put the white light back. It was a while before the first mechanical signals were introduced, with a bar and a disc set at right angles to each other on top of a pole. If the disc faced the driver, he was free to go ahead; if the bar was showing he had to stop. Things became more complex at junctions, where it was necessary to give right of way to one track or the other. There was just such a junction on the line from Greenwich to Croydon, where a branch line left the main road at Corbett's Lane. In order for the signalman to keep an eye out on all tracks he was provided with a hut on a platform. The signals used the same system as that used for hand signals – pointing down for all clear, horizontally for stop. It was the world's first signal box.

There was a disadvantage in the system. The clear signal was really no more than the absence of a visible signal – if the driver saw no warning sign, then he could assume everything was all right. Then on a wintry night in 1876 unknown to the signalman, when he thought he had pulled the lever that would move the signal from go to stop, nothing happened – it had frozen to the post. The result was a collision between an express and a slow goods train, that resulted in fourteen being killed and twenty-four seriously injured. As a result, the system was changed so that the clear sign was now visible as an arm pointing down at an angle, rather than hidden from view. A further development was the 'spectacle' attached to the arm, containing coloured glasses, that made the signal useable at night. As the arm swung, so an appropriate colour appeared in front of an oil lamp – so if the arm was set to danger, the red glass appeared in front of the lantern.

A major problem was the lack of any means of communication between signalmen up and down the line. William Fothergille Cooke, a former officer in the East India Army, devised a form of electric telegraph, which worked on the principal that a magnetic needle could be deflected by placing it near an electric wire when the current flowed. His first efforts were not entirely successful, but he was able to make improvements by seeking the assistance of one of the leading experts in electro-magnetism, Professor Charles Wheatstone of King's College, London. They formed a company to manufacture telegraph equipment, and in 1838 the Great Western installed a telegraph system between Paddington and West Drayton, later extending it to Slough. It was considered a great success and had a rather surprising part in the arrest of a murderer. A woman had been killed in Slough and the chief suspect had been spotted getting on a train for Paddington. His description was telegraphed ahead and when he reached London, the police were waiting.

Early signal boxes, such as this one of the 1850s, were mainly situated at junctions. Oil lamps for night signalling can be seen below the semaphore arms.

Thanks to the telegraph, the old system of separating trains by time could be replaced by the far more efficient block system. The block was the space between two sets of signals. When a train passed a signal box, a message would be sent to the next box down the line, and no train would be allowed into that block, until the first signalman got the word back that it had cleared the box. A further improvement was made when the pulling of a lever in the signal box to move a signal was automatically linked to the mechanism operating the points. The new system was summed up by its originator, John Saxby, in 1856:

> The semaphore signals, the coloured glasses of the signal lamps and the 'points' are all activated by a single motion of the lever, thus rendering the duties of the signalman of the most simple character and making it impossible for an accident to arise from the signals and the points differing.

This was the system that was to remain in place, with small variations, throughout the steam age. It helped to make train travel one of the safest, if not *the* safest, form of transport in the world. And, many would argue, one of the most enjoyable.

Chapter Six

The Underground

Surprisingly, the idea of constructing an underground railway for London was first put forward right at the start of the railway age in 1830. It originated with a campaigning lawyer, Charles Pearson, who had taken up a variety of radical causes, from the removal of the law denying the rights of Jews, to the disestablishment of the Church of England. He noticed that London's streets were becoming ever more crowded and saw this as a practical solution. The scheme was received with a mixture of fear and ridicule – fear that such a system would undermine houses and would see streets suddenly subsiding; while 'experts' declared the whole idea was absurd. However, the problem did not go away, and he found an ally in John Hargrave Stevens, who was to become the City architect and surveyor, and who was also an advocate for proper town planning. With the steady growth of railways, Pearson put his idea out again in a pamphlet of 1845. He proposed a line running down the line of the River Fleet to Farringdon. He suggested that it would be an atmospheric railway. We now know that atmospheric railways were far from successful, but in many ways, it was a sensible idea. It would have got rid of a major problem as the only alternative was working it with some sort of steam, with all that entailed in smoke and soot. That idea, too, failed to receive any real backing.

After being given an official role as the City Solicitor, he continued to promote the idea of an underground railway, and now proposed a new type of terminus at Farringdon that could be used by all the major railway companies as the main city station. The line to the north was to be in a deep cutting that would then be covered over. That too was rejected in spite of the support of the City. But the overcrowding of London streets was only getting worse, and Pearson continued to push for a new system, as he explained in the 'Railway Terminus and City Improvement Plan' of 1853. He identified a new phenomenon – the commuter.

> The overcrowding of the city is caused first by the natural increase in the population and area of the surrounding district; secondly

by the influx of provincial passengers by the great railways North of London, and the obstruction experienced in the streets by omnibuses and cabs coming from their distant stations to bring the provincial travellers to and from the heart of the city. I point next to the vast increase of what I may term the migratory population of the city who now oscillate between the country and the city, who leave the City of London every afternoon and return every morning.

The development of the main line stations of Paddington, Euston and King's Cross brought a great influx of traffic and it was eventually agreed that something had to be done. Various schemes were put forward, but the one which won the day was the Metropolitan Railway. It received its Act in 1854, allowing for a line that would link these three stations to Farringdon. Construction was in the hands of John Fowler (later Sir John) and the architect was Pearson's old ally, Stevens. The method of construction was the one first suggested by Pearson, digging a deep cutting, then covering it over, the process usually known simply as 'cut and cover'. If the construction of the London & Birmingham created chaos when it sliced through Camden Town, the Metropolitan created even more. It ran for 3¾ miles, and pedestrians who wanted to cross the deep trenches had to make do with simple plank bridges. The actual construction costs were estimated at between £50 and £60 a yard, but the costs in compensation for buildings that had to be destroyed or repaired were enormous. The damage to one chapel was estimated to cost £14,500 – the equivalent of over 250 yards of construction. There was one major accident when the River Fleet broke in, flooding the works, but fortunately no one was seriously injured and the damage was soon repaired.

Work had already begun when the Great Western put in a request that the tracks should be broad gauge so that they could use the line and offered to supply their own locomotives and carriages. This was agreed and was shortly followed by another request, this time from the Great Northern, for a third rail to allow their trains onto the track as well, and that too was agreed. The first engines used on the line, designed by Daniel Gooch, were broad gauge 2-4-0s with six-foot driving wheels and the coaches were eight-wheeled. The first short trial run took place on 24 May 1862, with two contractors' wagons fitted out with bench seats. It was a most curious sight, with the wagons packed with gentlemen in tall hats, including William Gladstone. It was a success, and on Saturday, 10 January 1863, the line opened to the general public. It was the world's first underground railway and attracted huge crowds eager to try this exciting new form of transport. Everyone, rich and poor alike, bought tickets on the first weekend, netting the company £850 – enough to pay half the cost for repairing the chapel.

Sharing the lines was always going to be a problem, and the Great Western was soon complaining about the service they were getting and threatening to withdraw both their locomotives and carriages if they weren't given a better share of the traffic. The Metropolitan called their bluff, by promptly hiring locomotives and carriages from the Great Northern, before beginning to plan to obtain their own rolling stock. John Fowler designed a locomotive that was quite unlike anything seen before. As well as the conventional firebox, there was also what was called a 'combustion chamber' filled with firebricks. On setting out, steam would be raised and the bricks heated. The engine was to work conventionally in the open,

The first select band of passengers, mostly shareholders, on the newly completed Metropolitan Railway did not exactly get VIP treatment, having to travel on benches in trucks.

but in tunnels, the firebox damper was closed down and heat was supplied from the heated bricks. Steam, instead of simply escaping into the atmosphere, was condensed and the water fed back to the boiler. It was known as 'Fowler's Ghost', as it was very quiet when running, but was not a success. Later engines were more conventional but reduced the smoke by using coke as a fuel and continued to condense the exhaust steam.

The underground was a great success, carrying around 10 million passengers in its first year, even though they enjoyed little in the way of comfort. Lighting was by gas, but was not very efficient, and although smoking was forbidden because of the fire risk, passengers often brought along their own candles so that they could see to read on the train. However, the success inevitably led to other new lines being opened. The Metropolitan was extended to Hammersmith, while a new company began the District Line, originally running from South Kensington to Westminster. By 1884, the District Line had been completed and the Metropolitan was reaching ever further from the centre.

The early lines were all cut and cover, and for ventilation had short shafts up to the surface. When a train ran through it sent a

The Metropolitan Railway was originally built to take both broad and standard gauge trains. In this illustration, both trains are broad gauge, but a third rail can be seen between the tracks for standard gauge.

THE UNDERGROUND • 117

A workers' early morning train on the Metropolitan. Originally the line was worked with steam locomotives.

The District Line under construction outside the Mansion House. Instead of tunnelling, the line was constructed by digging a deep cutting and then covering it over.

sudden gust of sooty air up to the street. If this happened when a young lady was crossing it could have an effect immortalized by Marilyn Monroe in the movie *The Seven Year Itch* when just such a gust sent her skirt flying high. The answer was to abandon cut and cover in favour of deeper tunnels. Peter Barlow was the first to suggest such a plan. He had a distinguished career as a civil engineer, having begun his working life with Cubitt on the South Eastern Railway and then becoming chief engineer for that line and railways in Ireland, as well as designing the Lambeth Bridge. It was while driving the cylinders into the riverbed so that men could work inside to build the central pier that he had the idea of using a series of horizontal iron cylinders to form a tube through which trains could run. It was not a new idea. Marc Brunel had suggested something very similar for the original Thames tunnel, though the idea was not used. In fact, the old Brunel tunnel had already been adapted for rail traffic, when it was bought by the East London Railway Company, who began running trains through it in 1869. Barlow did, however, suggest using an improved version of the tunnelling shield, in a circular version, to create his underground route. He proposed a tunnel under the Thames from Tower Hill to Southwark. The tube was to be 6ft 8in in diameter and was to take a 2ft 6in gauge track. There would be no locomotives, and just a single car holding twelve passengers would be hauled back and forth by cable from a stationary steam engine. The Tower Subway Company was formed and work began in 1869, with Barlow as chief engineer and James Henry Greathead as his assistant. Passengers paid a penny for a single fare. They reached the line by means of steam powered lifts. It was not a success. Lifts broke down, trains stopped and terrified passengers found themselves trapped, if only temporarily, either deep underground or, even worse, under the Thames. After just a few months, all the machinery and rails were removed and it became a pedestrian tunnel. That remained open but little used, and its fate was sealed when Tower Bridge was completed: no one wanted to walk through a narrow, dank tunnel, when they could walk across the river in the open air. The little tunnel did, however, find a practical use when pipes for the London Hydraulic Company were laid through it. It may not have had a long career as a transport system, but it was the first of the London tubes. It also encouraged Greatbatch to continue with the idea of tube trains.

He promoted a new company, the City of London & Southwark Subway Company, later known more simply as the City & South

London. Greatbatch had been very impressed by the San Francisco cable cars. These used a continuous looped cable, attached to huge rotating drums. Each car had a device underneath that could be clamped to the constantly moving cable and released when it needed to be braked. He planned a similar system for his new line under the Thames and had even begun ordering material, when a new technology appeared that offered a far better alternative. Werner Von Siemens had demonstrated the world's first electric locomotive at the Berlin Trade Exhibition of 1879. The little engine was brought to England in 1881. One man who saw it and was impressed was Magnus Volk, who built Britain's first electric railway along the sea front at Brighton in 1883. The plans for cable haulage were put on hold, while experiments were made with small electric locomotives in 1889.

The railway was being built long before anything like the national grid existed, so the company had to build their own power house at Stockwell. Originally it contained three 450hp compound

Early electric underground trains at Stockwell station. The locomotive can be seen on the left. The tiny windows high up in the carriage walls made the interior seem very claustrophobic and were later replaced by windows at passenger level.

steam engines that were used to turn Edison-Hopkins generators, which produced a DC electric current at 500 volts and 450 amps. The generators were a massive 17 tons each and rotated at 500rpm. The supply was fed to the locomotives through a third rail. Each locomotive pulled a train of three wooden carriages that seated thirty-two passengers, facing each other on bench seats. One of the coaches was reserved for smokers, but women were not allowed to use it. Sliding lattice doors at the end of the carriage were operated by gate men who also announced the name of the station, which was necessary as there were no windows, only ventilation slits high up near the roof. The company presumably felt that as there was nothing to see in the tube, there was no point in having windows. Upholstery ran high up the carriage walls and this, together with the claustrophobic atmosphere, led to the carriages being known as 'padded cells'. The grand opening by the Prince of Wales, later Edward VII, took place in November 1890 and in his speech, he praised 'the first electric railway in England' – which it wasn't – but it no doubt pleased the company directors. It was an immediate success, helped by the fact that passengers were charged a flat fare of just twopence, payable at the turnstile entrance. Over the next few years, the route was to be steadily extended, first north to the Angel and south to Clapham. In the early years of the twentieth century, there was a further extension to Euston. Over the next few years, the line was extended north and south and eventually in 1937 became part of London Underground's Northern Line.

The system began to spread and was constantly improved. The days of underground steam were coming to an end, and the most important change came when the District Railway built its new power station at Lots Road in Chelsea. Built in 1905, it was in its time the biggest power station for railways anywhere in the world.

The original eight Westinghouse generators rated at 5,500kW were fed by an array of boilers in the basement that were supplied with coal by barges on the Chelsea Creek. More electric trains were added over the years and one line offered a luxury that has certainly not been seen on the Tube since then. A number of small companies combined to form the London Electric Railway and they had two Pullman Cars on the line from the City, with comfortable armchairs and refreshments served at the tables. By this time, the Metropolitan line ran all the way out to Aylesbury and Amersham. The company needed to attract regular commuters into the city and it seemed that the best way to do that was to build affordable houses. They began work in 1919 and over the next few years they were to build a total of 4,600 houses, mostly in the mock Tudor style. Even new stations had a homely arts and crafts style. The company coined the name 'Metroland' to advertise their properties. Sir John Betjeman in his documentary *Metro-Land* summed up one of the stops on the line, Neasden, as 'home of the gnome and the average citizen'. It was a phrase that could be applied to much of Metroland, but the houses were well built, comfortable and affordable. And they did what they were meant to do – bring in the commuters.

One of the problems that faced the developers of the system was getting the passengers between the platforms and the surface. This was solved on 4 October 1911 when the first escalators were introduced at Earl's Court Station, both built by a company famous

The Lots Road power station built to provide electricity for the District Railway Company in 1897.

The preserved electric locomotive *Sarah Siddons*, built in 1921 by Metropolitan Vickers for the Metropolitan Railway.

for lifts, Otis. There had been a number of attempts to provide some form of moving staircase, including a spiral version installed at Holloway Road tube, which was never brought into use. The modern escalator is based on a design by the American Charles Seeberger, who joined forces with Otis to develop his design. To allay fears about safety, the company hired a man with a wooden leg, 'Bumper' Harris, to travel up and down. In spite of that, there were a few accidents in the first week, including nine torn dresses and a man who fell off his crutches. Following that, a guard rail was added and the system was declared a resounding success. Today, it is impossible to imagine the system working without its escalators. They had a splendid safety record until the night of 18 November 1987, when a fire started on the wooden escalator on the Piccadilly Line escalator at King's Cross, thought to have been caused by someone dropping a lighted match. It seemed a minor affair, until there was a sudden flashover and flames shot into the booking hall. Altogether, thirty-one people died that night and a hundred were injured.

Safety on the Underground was efficiently secured as early as the first decade of the twentieth century, when a new signalling system was adopted. When a train passed a clear sign, it automatically switched to danger. This was improved on shortly afterwards when the signals were connected to a track circuit. If a driver failed to see a stop sign, then an automatic train stop on the track would bring it to a halt. When the locomotives were abandoned in favour of the type of train we know today, with its motor controlled by the driver alone in his cab at the front, a new problem arose. What happened if the driver collapsed for some reason? The answer took the form of a device who took its name from the worst possible scenario – the dead man's handle. The driver had to keep constant pressure on the handle, or the train stopped. He could, in theory, slump down onto the handle, allowing the train to thunder on, but he also had to press a foot pedal to keep going. All these safety devices have combined to make the Underground a remarkably safe way to travel.

By the outbreak of the First World War, the Underground network was all but complete. Extensions further out into the suburbs, in the post-war years, were mainly overground. The Northern line extension, however, was still largely underground and Morden became the most southerly station on the underground system and the line from East Finchley is still the longest tunnel on the system. The new stations were designed by Charles Holden in a modernist style that has become known as Art Deco. Much of the new network would seem quite familiar to modern travellers. Trains with automatic sliding doors were introduced onto the Piccadilly line, which was also extended and, like the Northern line, acquired new, architect-designed stations. In 1932, the iconic Arnos Grove station was opened, and at once became recognized as a fine example of modern architecture, with its simple drum shaped entrance hall. Charles Holden was again the architect and he opted for simplicity and modern materials. Refurbishment in 2005 kept the distinctive features of the original building. It now has a Grade II* listing, which should ensure its survival.

One major difference between then and now, was that the system was still run by a mixture of different independent companies. That changed in 1933 when the running of the system was taken over by the London Passenger Transport Board. The old companies received

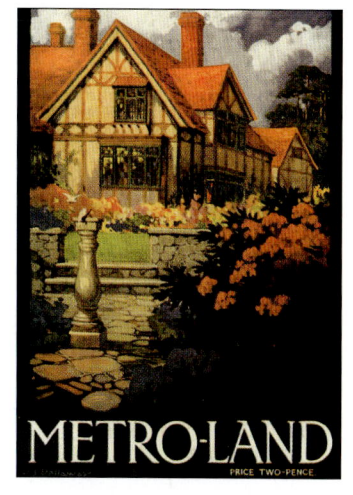

Thanks to the extension of the Metropolitan Railway, whole new suburbs were developed with houses based on the ideals of the Arts and Crafts movement, and the area came to be known as Metroland.

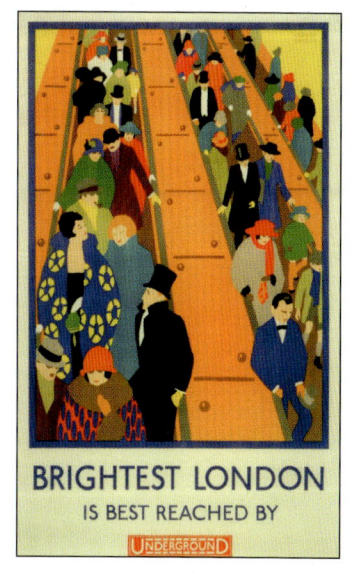

Escalators were first introduced to the Underground in the early twentieth century and were sufficiently novel to be featured on posters.

compensation, but no longer had any say in the running of the system. Then, when war broke out in 1939, the government took control of the whole rail system including the Underground, and one of the changes they made was to make tubes a single class as they have remained ever since. Famously, the Tubes came to be used as air raid shelters. They were not quite the safe havens everyone had expected. In October 1940, a bomb burst through the tunnel at Balham, bursting the water main and deluging the station, killing sixty-nine people. The following January another bomb hit Bank station, and the road above collapsed down onto the platforms resulting in 56 deaths and many injuries.

The original ornate entrance to what was then Trafalgar Square tube station, now known as Charing Cross.

The splendid Art Deco octagonal booking hall at Morden tube station.

The first major new work after the war was begun in 1962 with the construction of the Victoria Line. By this time, tunnelling technology had moved forward, and a giant machine, known as the Drum Digger, moved forward automatically, chewing away at the ground, while in its wake the tube sections were lowered into place. It was a highly sophisticated line with automatic trains, though they still had a driver in the cab. The carriages were an improvement with double glazed windows, which cut out much of the noise of the train, and the driver was able to communicate directly with the control centre. There were closed circuit television cameras installed at all the stations, and automatic ticket machines were introduced.

The Jubilee line was opened in 1979, between Stratford and Stanmore, part of it along former Metropolitan tracks. It was not particularly innovative, but the same cannot be said for the Jubilee Extension. There had been talk of extending the line for some time, but the real need for it only appeared pressing with the Canary Wharf development, which brought a new wave of commuters to the large office development on the Isle of Dogs.

In the Second World War, Londoners crowded into the Underground at night to avoid the bombing.

A forerunner of the modern tube map. Instead of being purely diagrammatic, it gives an indication of where the stations are in relation to the city above ground.

Construction began in 1993 and the whole line was finally opened in December 1999 in time for what was hoped to be the vast crowds visiting the Millennium Dome across the river in North Greenwich. For the first time since the Thirties, underground stations were architect designed, this time with Roland Paoletti as the chief architect. Each station has its own character, but all share a common theme. They are spacious, with entrances that are naturally lit and everything is a sleek modernity of steel, glass and concrete. Soon after opening, I made a trip on the extension, stopping off at each station on the line just to admire the architecture. Soon it will not be the latest link in the Underground, as Crossrail are constructing the Elizabeth line, from Reading and Heathrow to Shenfield and Abbey Wood, a total of 42km of new tunnels. It will be interesting to see if the new stations have the same architectural qualities as the Jubilee Extension.

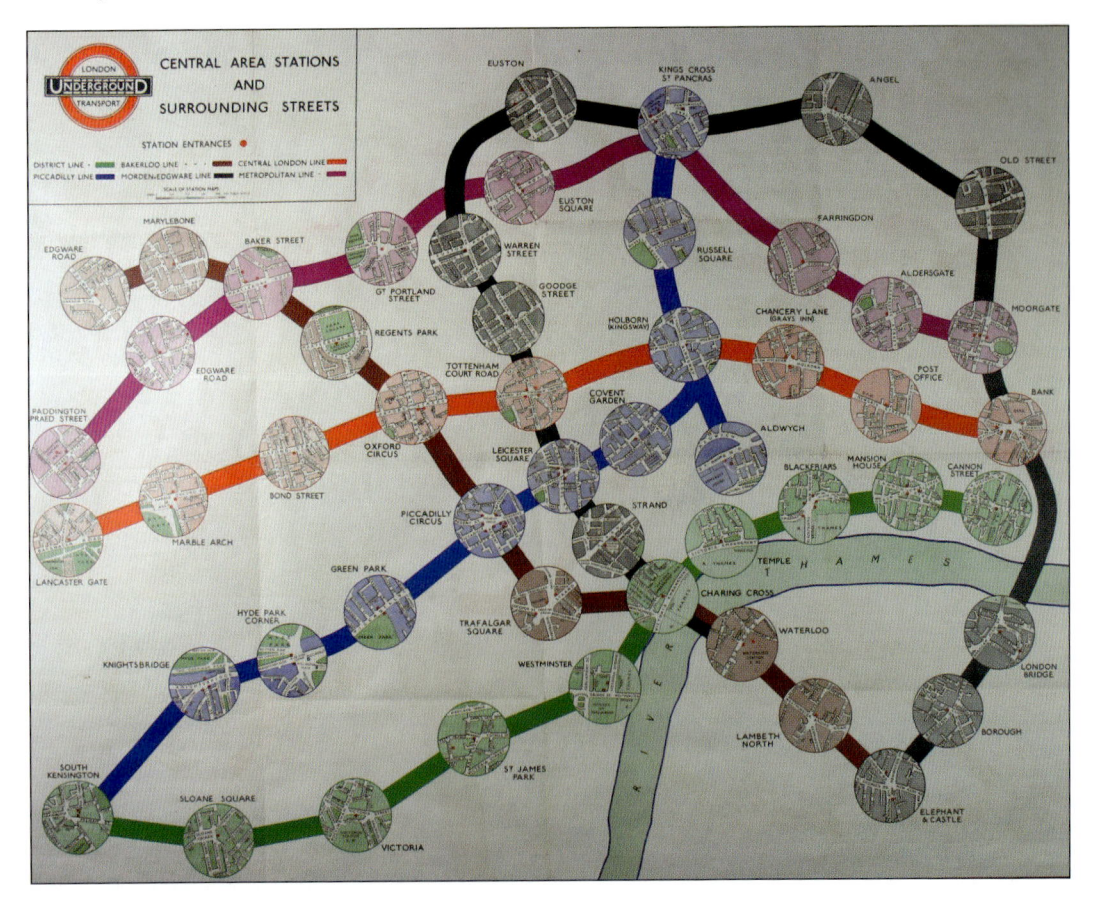

One element has remained constant on the London Underground since 1933, the tube map designed by Harry Beck. Older cartographers had treated tube maps just as they would if asked to produce a road map – showing every twist and turn and accurately reproducing distances between stations. Beck's genius lay in recognizing this was unnecessary. It made no difference to the tube traveller if the lines to his next stop went round curves or ran straight, and distances were irrelevant. All the traveller needed to know was how to get from his starting point to his destination with whatever changes were necessary in between. So, everything was simplified right down and, although since then new lines and new stations have been added, the overall design is still the same. It is such a familiar part of London life, that we take it for granted. Where would London be without the tube, and how would we ever get round it without the help of Beck's map? But the tube is not the only way of getting around the city, and by the start of the twentieth century, a new form of transport was appearing on London streets.

CHAPTER SEVEN

Trams and Trolleys

By the middle of the nineteenth century, horse drawn omnibuses were becoming a common sight on the streets of London. However, it was obvious that overcrowding was an increasing problem. One possible solution was to increase the size of the omnibus so that it could take more passengers. That literally required more horse power. Right at the beginning of the century, the engineers Thomas Telford and John Smeaton had carried out a series of experiments to show the load that could be shifted by a single horse. As canal engineers, they were obviously producing evidence to show the superiority of water transport, but they also showed that while a horse could pull two tons on a well-made macadam road, it could haul eight tons if the wagon was run on a railed track. Tramways were already in use for hauling freight in many parts of Britain, including London, where the Surrey Iron Railway had enjoyed a brief existence. But they were nearly all limited to moving freight, not people. Now, however, there seemed to be a case for urban tramways to help relieve congestion. The *Railway Times* was, not surprisingly, an early supporter of the idea, writing an editorial on the subject as early as 1843, but to no effect.

The first real effort to create a tramway system for the capital was put forward by the London General Omnibus Co. (LGOC) in 1857, for a line from Notting Hill Gate to the Bank with a branch line from Fleet Street to King's Cross. The Company had been formed originally as an Anglo-French concern, though rather more French than English it seems, as it was first called Compagnie Generale des Omnibus de Londres in 1855. It had first been set up to bring together the various small omnibus companies to provide some sort of order to the system, but quickly recognized the advantage of tramways. However, the tramway plans were opposed by other passenger road companies and individuals who simply objected to the whole idea of modernisation.

The rather appropriately named George Francis Train was born in Boston, Massachusetts in 1829 and was an entrepreneur who was fascinated by modern transport systems. In 1853, he moved to

Australia, as agent for the White Diamond shipping line, but was always on the lookout for new ideas and new places to try them. In Melbourne, he had been responsible for building warehouses on the railway linking the docks to the city centre. Perhaps it was seeing how the line improved the movement of passengers that reminded him of conversations he had had at school with a boy who had emigrated from Birkenhead who told him of the transport difficulties of his old hometown. In any case, he arrived in England and inaugurated Europe's first street tram system at Birkenhead. Encouraged by this success, he moved to London to promote the idea. He was successful and his first tramway opened on 23 March 1861 along the Bayswater Road from Marble Arch to Porchester Terrace, opposite Kensington Gardens. It was considered very successful by those who used it, but a good deal less so by other road users. The problem was the rails, raised above the road surface. People tripped over them, vehicles had to bump over them if they tried to turn off the main road and one cab driver reported that his cab had caught the rails and his horse had somersaulted into the air and landed on its back. The nuisance was too great and within months of opening, all Train's rails had been removed. He returned to America where he was soon busy setting up the Union Pacific Railway, a vital link in that country's first transcontinental line.

An early horse omnibus run by the London General Omnibus Company. Vehicles of this type were in use up to 1914.

Nine years went by without any further progress, but 1870 saw a flurry of activity, with gangs of men track-laying in many parts of the city. The first to open was a line from Brixton to Kennington on 2 May of that year, followed just a week later by a line from Whitechapel to Bow, built for the North Metropolitan Tramways Co., who were to go on to become London's busiest tram operators for many years. The Brixton-Kennington line was extended to Westminster in October and the year's activity ended with a line from New Cross to Blackheath, opened on 13 December. J. Joyce, in his history of London trams, records one satisfied customer as reporting that he was impressed by the smooth running and comfort of the trams. 'A dozen portly people may sit comfortably upon broad-cushioned seats with stuffed backs along each side of the vehicle, and have a clear space of a foot-and-a-half between their knees along the centre'. Other citizens were less enthusiastic, especially those living close to the tracks, where the rattle of iron wheels on iron rails made for a noisy environment. But the system kept on growing so that by the 1890s there were 14 companies operating over 130 miles of track, stretching out as far as Epping Forest in the east and Richmond in the west and carrying some 200 million passengers a year.

While steam locomotives were puffing their way in and out of London, the trams were still being pulled by horses. It must have

A horse tram of c.1900. By running on rails instead of on the rough road, the trams could carry more passengers than the horse buses.

seemed sensible to replace the horse by a light steam engine. The first to build a steam powered tram was John Grantham in 1872. The engine was in the centre, with a covered compartment for twenty passengers inside and twenty-four in the open top. It was given its first trial run early the following year between Victoria Station and Vauxhall Bridge, but was not a great success as the small boiler was unable to keep up the steam pressure. It was sent off to the Wantage Tramway, where it suffered from the same problem, and also had difficulty rounding the sharp tramway curves. However, once its overall length had been reduced from 30ft to 27ft 3in and a new boiler installed, it proved a great success and remained in use for many years. The North London Tramway Co. persevered with a more conventional form of steam power, with trailers pulled by a small locomotive between 1885 and 1891.

Another form of traction for trams was first conceived in 1869 when Andrew Smith Hallidie saw an omnibus slip on a steep hill in San Francisco, overturning and killing the horses. To overcome the problem, he developed the famous street cars. A loop of steel cable is kept in constant motion by giant rotating wheels. The power car has a mechanism that can grip the cable to move forward and release again when it needs to stop. The system was adopted for use on Highgate Hill – not quite as spectacular as San Francisco – in 1884 and remained in use until 1909. A similar system was also installed at Streatham in 1892.

A steam omnibus. The engine is in the central compartment but vehicles of this type were never a great success in London.

Cable cars, similar to those pioneered in San Francisco, ran for a time in London

The real breakthrough in technology this time came from Germany, where the world's first electric tramway was opened in 1884, running between Frankfurt-am-Main and Offenbach. The power was supplied from overhead cables in slotted pipes with lugs poking through the bottom, which could be attached by light frames and cables to the motor in the power car. In 1885, Britain got its first electric tram, not in London, but in the seaside resort of Blackpool. Originally, the electric supply came from a conduit between the rails: trams powered by overhead cables first ran in Leeds in 1891. Other towns followed suit, but the capital still lagged behind, although an experimental line was laid out in the grounds of Alexandra Palace in 1898. London had to wait for the start of the twentieth century before the city streets saw their first electric tram.

The London United Tramways Company was formed in 1894 and took over the old West Metropolitan Co. tracks, which were operated by horse trams. Once they had decided on electrification, they had to build a generating station at Chiswick and replace the old track. The first trials took place at night in February 1901, starting at Chiswick and covering the route between Hammersmith and Kew. By 4 April, everything was considered to be satisfactory and the first public services were opened with routes from Hammersmith and from Shepherd's Bush to Kew Bridge and from

Shepherd's Bush to Acton. There was a short branch from Kew Green to Richmond, but that was still operated by horse trams as Kew Bridge was too narrow to take the new vehicles. Even when the bridge was rebuilt in 1903, permission to cross it was refused, largely because of opposition from locals who objected to what they regarded as unsightly overhead wires. The horse buses remained in use right up to 1912. The official opening was delayed until July, by which time the route had been extended to Southall and Hounslow. It was a grand affair, with nine tramcars, garlanded with flowers, taking the guests over the route, followed by a lunch at the Chiswick generating station. The trams were described as 'very handsome', which indeed they were as can be seen in the photo below. They were double-deckers, with bench seats on the lower level, and an open top with an ornate balustrade.

The existing London tramways had all been run by a hotch-potch of different companies and local authorities began to think that they could best serve their communities by having their own systems designed to meet local needs. Between 1901 and 1906, five local

A London United electric tram preserved in the London Transport Museum.

London trams ran on two different systems, taking power from overhead lines or from live rails beneath the road. Here at Brixton, the two systems met. The tram is attached to the overhead lines, and the pick up for the underground power source has just been removed.

authorities set up municipal tramways, starting with East Ham and Croydon. These two authorities led the way and it was only after they had proved successful that the biggest local authority of them all, the London County Council (LCC), decided to join in. They, however, were concerned that the overhead supply system would detract from the dignity and beauty of the city, so decided to use the conduit system. This is essentially the same as the original overhead system used in Germany, except that the live conductor rails were buried underground, with a lug poking up through the slot to connect to the car. It kept the city streets clear of poles and wires but cost twice as much to install. The opening of the new routes was by far the grandest of any of the opening ceremonies. The passengers of honour were the Prince and Princess of Wales, later to be George V and Queen Mary, and their two sons, Edward and George, who would also be crowned later. It is doubtful if any other form of transport had ever carried three future kings of England at the same time. Two other major companies opened lines in the first decade of the twentieth century – the Metropolitan Electric Tramways in 1904 and the South Metropolitan Tramways & Lighting Co. in 1906.

The network was soon spreading across most of London, but the LCC had a problem in that they were operating one set of trams on a northern section and another set to the south, but they would ideally have liked to unite them so that they could all be serviced at the same depot at Charlton. It was decided that the only way to achieve this was to go underground in a subway that would link Theobalds Road in Holborn to the embankment at Waterloo Bridge. After four years of legal wrangling, permission to build what was to become the Kingsway Subway was granted in 1906. The authorities, however, refused permission for the trams to cross the bridge. That was a disappointment, but the subway was built, linking in to a new line along the embankment. The ramp at the Holborn end was quite steep and in the early days, trams leaving Holborn station would stutter towards the top of the slope only to roll back down again. Although originally built to take only single-decker trams, it was enlarged in 1929 to take double-deckers.

The trams were an undoubted success. By 1914, there were 2,898 trams in the London area, of which 1,778 were operated by the LCC and between them they carried over 800 million passengers a year. After the end of the First World War, there was an ominous sign for tram operators with the appearance of the motor bus, which we shall look at in the next chapter. One response was to replace the old trams with trolley buses, getting rid of the rails and running on rubber-tyred wheels. The first trolleys, known as 'Diddlers', were built for London United Transport in 1931. After just two years in operation, they were taken over by the London Passenger Transport Board together with all the tram companies.

A tram emerging from the Kingsway underpass.

It began a steady programme of replacing all the trams with trolley buses and by the start of the war in 1939 all the north London tramways had been converted, though south London still had a thousand trams in use. However, the days of the trolley bus were numbered as they were steadily replaced by diesel buses. The last trolley bus ran on 8 May 1962.

That would have seemed to be the end of the story as far as trams and trolleys were concerned as they gave way to the familiar red diesel buses. By the end of the twentieth century, however, pollution from diesel fumes had become an increasingly worrying phenomenon and already there were dire warnings about the effects on global warming. Electric trams no longer seemed an anachronism, but a solution. Several schemes were put forward for a tramway system based on Croydon to serve surrounding suburbs and in particular providing a link to New Addington that had been developed in the post-war years. In 1990, Croydon Council and London Regional Transport combined to present a scheme called Tramlink to parliament. An Act was passed in 1994 and in 2000 the new system opened with 39km of track, not just to New Addington

Trolley buses in Islington in the 1950s.

but westward to Wimbledon and east to Beckenham, with a branch to Elmers End. The trams themselves were built by Bombardier, based on the design first developed for the Cologne State Railway system. They are articulated and have low floors for easy access direct from the platforms. In a neat historic twist, part of the route between Mitcham and Hackbridge follows the line of London's first tramway, the Surrey Iron Railway, built two centuries earlier.

Modern Tramlink trams at Croydon.

Chapter Eight

Motor Vehicles

Motor vehicles fell into two distinct categories. There were those built for individuals that would soon take over from the horse and carriage for the rich, though it would be some time before anyone else could afford them. The others were designed for public transport.

The first motor vehicle to take to the streets of London was a taxi cab driven by an electric motor. Designed by a brilliant 23-year-old engineer, Walter Charles Bersey, it made its first run in August 1897. Bersey formed the London Electric Cab Company, and some seventy of the vehicles were soon running. They suffered, however, from one serious disadvantage. To provide the power, they required massive batteries, each weighing in at around three quarters of a ton. The immense weight put a great strain on the wheels and rapidly wore out the rubber tyres. They were not a success, and only lasted a couple of years before the company was dissolved. Others, however, soon took up the electric car idea. The Electromobile was manufactured in Britain and was distributed on hire from a vast garage in Mayfair. Hirers had no need to recharge batteries – they simply brought the car back and had the old one replaced. The company survived and remained in business right up to the 1920s. Electric cars of that period never really overcame the problem of the heavy battery and short distances that could be travelled. They succumbed to another new form of power, the internal combustion engine.

The idea of the internal combustion engine was not new. As early as 1680, the Dutch scientist Christian Huygens had proposed an engine which involved exploding gunpowder in a cylinder with a piston. The expanding hot gases, together with some of the air originally in the tube would be allowed to escape through valves that would close as the piston cooled. The result would be a partial vacuum in the cylinder and air pressure would force the piston down. The biggest problem with the system was the difficulty involved in constantly refilling the cylinder with gunpowder, not to mention the danger of blowing up the user of such a device. The theory was sound, but it was impossible to make it work

The first motorized London cab, the Bersey electric taxi.

in practice. With the success of steam power, interest in internal combustion faded away until the nineteenth century.

The new development was the gas engine, with coal gas as the fuel instead of gunpowder. There were early experiments at the beginning of the nineteenth century, but the first successful model was designed by the French engineer Etienne Lenoir in 1859. As with steam engines of the time, it relied on the expansion of hot gases acting on either side of the piston to work and used an electric spark to ignite the air-gas mixture. There was one big improvement made by Nicolaus Otto, whose engine followed a specific cycle – admission of gas, compression, ignition, expansion (the power stroke) and exhaust. The Otto gas engine was so successful that 50,000 of the 4 horsepower version were sold in the seventeen years after its introduction in 1876. It was a highly efficient machine but rooted to the spot simply because it had to be attached to a source of gas. But it had established the efficiency of both internal combustion and the Otto cycle. All that was needed was a more suitable fuel, and the answer was of course found to be petroleum-based fluids – petrol or diesel.

Although they were not the first to attempt to use internal combustion engines in vehicles, there are two pioneers whose work really did change the whole world of land transport, Karl Benz and Gottlieb Daimler. Benz's first vehicle of 1885 was a three-wheeled car with a horizontal single-cylinder petrol engine. As with the Trevithick steam coach, the single front wheel was steered with a tiller. The inventor was reluctant to take the machine out for any long journeys, but his wife Bertha was an intrepid and resourceful woman. Without telling her husband, she decided to drive for 106km from their home in Mannheim to visit her mother in Pforzheim. Several things went wrong en route – she ran out of fuel and bought paraffin at a pharmacist and when the fan belt broke, she replaced it with her garter. In later developments, Benz moved on to bigger four-wheel cars. Gottlieb Daimler's contribution was the first high-speed internal combustion engine; a single cylinder version was used for the world's first motorcycle in 1886. A similar engine was later installed in a four wheeled carriage. As other manufacturers began to produce models, cars began to race each other. A fast car was ordered from Daimler and it proved very successful. Others wanted similar cars and asked for them under the name of the original – it had been called Mercedes after the owner's daughter. Eventually, Daimler merged with Benz and that is how the Mercedes Benz became known.

Britain was slow to develop the motor car and though Edward Butler built a motorised tricycle in 1887, he never followed it up, mainly because of the so-called 'Red Flag Act', which limited powered vehicles to a speed of 2mph in towns and 4mph in the country. This was increased to 12mph by an Act of 1896, which still referred to road vehicles as 'locomotives', because they were steam powered. Further increases came with the Motor Car Act of 1903. Nine years after Butler's experiment, Frederick Lanchester set about building a car that he designed from first principles, rather than simply thinking in terms of sticking an engine in a carriage to replace the horse. It was a success, though underpowered, and a second version was built with an 8hp engine in place of the original 5hp version. It was the start of a successful business that he established in Birmingham. London engineers had not yet considered car manufacturing, but that began to change in the early years of the twentieth century.

First into the field were James and Browne, who had their factory in King's Street, between Hammersmith and Chiswick. They were said to have first made a car in 1899, but the earliest recorded model, and the first to be built from the new factory, appeared in 1901. A 1902 car

JAMES AND BROWNE
Petrol Propelled Bonnetless Landaulettes.

STAND No. 81.

THE IDEAL TOWN MOTOR CARRIAGE.

By our unique patented device the Motor is started from the driver's seat. Guaranteed absolutely free from smoke and smell. All mechanical parts most accessible. Small Turning Circle. The Chassis has recently been entirely re-designed, embodying many unique improvements.

THE J. and B. "VERTEX" (Regd.)

In response to public demand, we are now placing on the market our "J. & B. Vertex" Chassis of our own manufacture, fitted with six-cylinder vertical motor, embodying all modern improvements, coupled with the renowned J. & B. workmanship and materials; the prices will be found extremely moderate, while the quality is unsurpassed. Inspection cordially invited.

BRITISH BUILT BY BRITISH WORKMEN.

JAMES and BROWNE, LTD., Showrooms:—395, Oxford Street, LONDON, W.
WESTCROFT WORKS, HAMMERSMITH, LONDON, W.

James & Browne were the first car manufacturers to set up a business in London. The design is very much a horseless carriage.

still survives as does a later model of 1904. The design was original, with two horizontal cylinders, with a total capacity of approximately 2.5 litres and a flywheel in between. The gear box was split in two with second and fourth gear on the left and first, third and reverse on the right, linked by a sliding shaft. The drive was by a pair of chains and it was fitted with acetylene lamps. By 1906, they had introduced four-cylinder horizontal engines and were offering cars with up to 30hp. The first vertical engine car, the Vertex, was available in an even more powerful version, with a six-cylinder engine of 30/40hp. The company did not survive the First World War.

Not all the early cars were built by newly founded companies. One famous name has its origins in a company founded in 1857 by a Scottish engineer, Alexander Wilson. They occupied the site of the former Vauxhall Pleasure Gardens on the south bank of the Thames and became the Vauxhall Iron Works. They specialised in building marine steam engines, but in the late 1890s they produced a single cylinder petrol engine that was installed in a tiny river launch, the *Jabberwock*. It is generally accepted that the success of this small venture was the inspiration for moving on to manufacturing motor cars. By this time, Alexander Wilson had left the company, and his role was taken by F.W. Hodges, a marine engineer trained by Wilson, and J.H. Chambers. The first car appeared in 1903, a modest 5hp model with a single horizontal cylinder. It had tiller steering, and the throttle control was on the tiller arm. It had just two forward gears and no reverse, which must have made driving quite interesting. Nevertheless, the little car was capable of speeds up to 25mph. The first model was a two-seater, but a four-seater version was available, in which the passengers sat in front of the driver, over the engine, facing forward. Apart from obscuring the driver's view, the passengers must have felt decidedly vulnerable. The basic model cost £136. The following year, a 6 horsepower version appeared, but for some reason the wire-spoked wheels of the first version were replaced by solid wooden ones. At least the new one had a reverse gear.

This was a time when the car manufacturers were eager to prove the reliability of this new form of transport. Special events were organised and in October 1903, Vauxhall entered a car in the Hermitage Hill climb in the Scottish Borders, organised by the Wolverhampton and District Automobile Club, which they successfully completed. The following year they took part in the run from Glasgow to London. This was a reliability trial not a race, with points deducted for any failure of any part of the car along the way. Theirs was the smallest car in the competition but acquitted itself magnificently. Each car started with a score of 1,000 and the Vauxhall only lost 7 points on the whole journey. As well as good publicity, it was a valuable test of the equipment, and as a result a few changes were made, of which the most important was the abandonment of the awkward tiller in favour of the steering wheel. By this time, the company was also offering some weather protection as an extra. A simple overhead canopy – rather like the surrey with the fringe on top of *Oklahoma* - was available for 7 guineas and a leather hood for 16 guineas.

The Vauxhall Company had its works on the site of the old Vauxhall Pleasure Gardens. This is their 1903 model.

Success created new problems. The London factory was now short of space, and there were problems over extending the lease. As a result, the company left London for a new factory in Luton. The company was taken over by General Motors in the 1920s but continued manufacturing at Luton.

In the early years, it made sense for would be car manufacturers to set up business in London, since the capital was the place where there were the largest numbers of potential buyers who could actually afford to buy the vehicles. One of the most famous names among British car manufacturers began in London, named after its founder W.O. Bentley. He was born in 1888 and showed a precocious interest in engineering – he apparently took a bicycle to pieces to see how it worked when aged only eight. He was brought up in the age of steam, and left school at sixteen to take an apprenticeship with the Great Northern Railway, but his initial enthusiasm for steam locomotives eventually gave way to an interest in the new developments on the road. In 1907, he bought a Quadrant motorcycle – the first Quadrant had appeared in 1903 and gained a great deal of popularity following a well-advertised run from John O'Groats to Land's End. He and his two brothers took up racing. W.O., as he was always known, was successful in several

This model was the last Vauxhall to be built in London before the company moved to Luton.

trials, starting with a gold in the London-Edinburgh run, in spite of breaking down en route and having to make his own repairs. But he was not satisfied with merely riding bikes. He later changed from the Quadrant to the Rex motorcycle and set about making his own improvements to the engine, so successfully that the changes were adopted by the official Rex race team.

By 1912, he had left the Great Northern and set up in business with his brothers, importing Doriot, Fiandrin & Parant (DFP) cars from France. He visited the company's French headquarters in 1913, where he picked up a paperweight made of aluminium. That set him wondering whether this lighter metal might be a useful alternative to heavy iron for casting pistons. In order to increase its resistance to high temperatures, he experimented with various alloys, eventually settling for one containing 12 per cent copper. He used the new alloy pistons in a DFP car which he raced at Brooklyn, where he achieved a world record speed for a flying mile of 88.7mph This gave him the idea that he might go into car construction and develop the idea of using aluminium. Those plans came to an abrupt halt with the start of the First World War. His new ideas, however, were not wasted. He joined the Royal Naval Air Service, where he introduced his aluminium pistons into fighter planes. His rotary engine, the BR1, was installed in the Sopwith Camel biplane, generally recognised as the most successful British fighter of the war years. His experience in engine construction was to be put to good use when the war ended.

As a reward for his work during the war, he was awarded £8,000 by the Commission of Awards, enough for him to start Bentley Motors at Cricklewood in North London in July 1919. He famously declared, 'We are going to make a fast car, a good car, the best in its class.' It was not an idle boast, for he was to achieve his goal. *Autocar* magazine described the Bentley ideal as 'a true racing car with touring accessories'. A succession of ever more powerful cars followed, staring with a 3 litre engine, followed by the six cylinder 4½ litre in 1927 and the six cylinder 8 litre in 1930. The cars were to receive international recognition when they competed in the famous Le Mans 24-hour race, though Bentley himself was at first reluctant to enter. He changed his mind when a privately entered 3 litre Bentley finished fourth in 1923. The following year, Bentley came first. For the next two years, the cars failed to finish, but from 1927 to 1930 they dominated the race, taking first place each year and reaching a pinnacle of success in 1929 when the 4½ litre took the first four places. It was all magnificent publicity.

Bentley's ambition was to create a road car that would be silent and capable of speeds of 100 miles an hour. He achieved it with the

This magnificent machine is a 4½ litre Bentley fitted with a supercharger.

8 litre car, which was available in a variety of different body styles. The company simply noted that whatever style the owner chose, it would still be capable of doing the ton. The timing, however, was unfortunate. The Wall Street crash of 1929 sent economies plummeting, and the demand for high performance, very expensive cars dropped just as quickly. Only about 100 of these magnificent cars were made. The company's fortunes were crumbling and when their chief financial supporter, the Kimberley diamond magnate Barney Barnato, withdrew his support, the company went into liquidation. In November 1931, Bentley Motors was taken over by Rolls-Royce and production moved to Crewe. The days of the London Bentley were ended.

One other famous name entered the motoring annals, Napier. David Napier had been one of the leading developers of steam power for ships and it was his grandson Montague, born in 1870, who set the company in a new direction. He was an enthusiastic racing cyclist and it was at the Bath Road Club that he met S.F. Edge who was then manager at Dunlop. Edge owned a Panhard car and he persuaded Napier to convert it from tiller steering to steering wheel. Napier obliged him, but then went a step further. He suggested that he could build a better engine as well. Edge was impressed and encouraged Napier to begin manufacturing cars, while Edge and a partner set up the Motor Power Company in London, agreeing to take all the Napier cars and sell them from their showroom.

Where Bentley had made his name with the endurance race at Le Mans, Napier went for speed on the racing circuit. In June 1900, the first Napier was entered for the Paris-Toulouse-Paris race. Given the nature of the route and the comparative unreliability of the early cars, a travelling mechanic was taken along to try and fix anything that went wrong. He was a 22-year-old called Charles Rolls, who four years later was to meet Frederick Royce and form one of the most famous partnerships in motoring history. In 1901, Napier built a monstrously big car with a massive 16 litre engine. Only a few were ever built. By 1903 they were turning out 250 cars a year and formed a new company 'D. Napier and Son' and moved from their old site in Lambeth to new, larger premises in Acton in West London. Racing continued to be an important part of the Napier activities, and although they only continued running their own cars until 1908, they were later to supply engines for Malcolm Campbell's famous Blue Bird cars of 1927 and 1931.

S.F. Edge, who went into partnership to set up the Napier car company, in a 16hp Napier.

At the outbreak of war in 1914, they were making around 700 cars a year, but now production was shifted to making army trucks and ambulances. After the war, car production resumed, but the company began another change of course, when they started concentrating on aero-engines. Car production had ended by the start of the Second World War.

The arrival of the motor car did, of course, present a problem for the old coach builders, but a number took the successful 'If you can't beat them, join them' approach. One of these was Barker and Co., originally founded in London in 1710. The luxury car market usually offered customers a choice of bodywork and Barker finished up doing a great deal of such work for Rolls-Royce, who only started producing their own bodywork in 1946. Hooper's was another coach builder, very successful in the nineteenth century, who turned to the luxury car market, which was so successful that they had to extend their site on the Kings Road in 1911 and in 1938 they took over their main rivals Barker. These two companies between them produced some of the most elegant cars ever seen on British roads.

If the motor car posed a threat to carriage makers, it was even worse news for the owners of horse-drawn cabs. As early as 1905, Vauxhall were offering what they called a Motor Hansom, and over the next few years a whole range of motor taxis were being

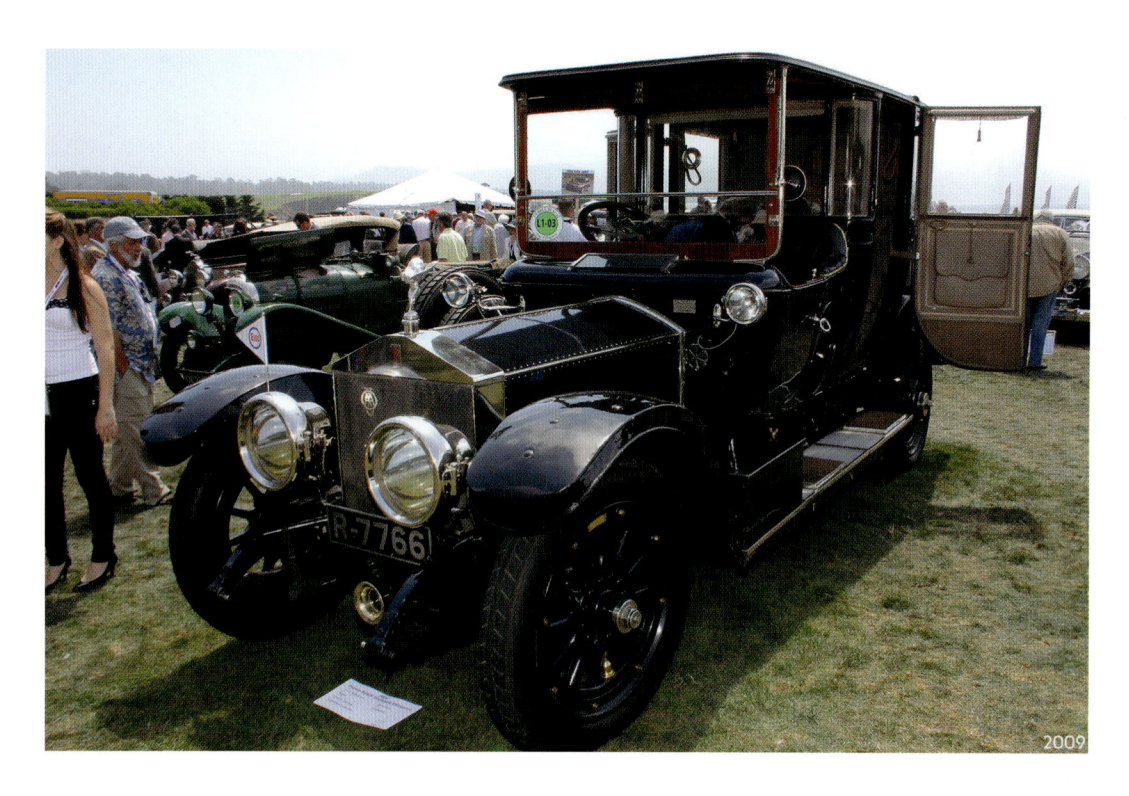

A 1913 Rolls-Royce Silver Ghost with body work by the old established London carriage makers, Baxter.

offered for sale and appeared on the streets of London. Even the French got in the act, offering the Unic range of taxis, that proved extremely popular and one of these vehicles is now preserved at the National Motor Museum at Beaulieu. One of the biggest names in the business was Austin, whose first effort of 1906 was not licensed, but an improved version appeared the following year. Ten of them were bought by the Taxi De Luxe Company of Kensington. The name 'taxi' told potential passengers that the cabs were fitted with taximeters, which would automatically display the correct fare and distance travelled. Austin would later go on to develop a whole range of taxis over the years.

In order to operate, taxis had to meet a set of standards first set out by the Public Carriage Office in 1906. One of the distinguishing features of all London cabs was the tight circle. This was officially set as no larger than 28 feet. It was not an arbitrary figure but was decided purely on the fact that this was necessary for the cabs to get round the roundabout at the front of the Savoy Hotel. Clearly it was important for those staying at this exclusive hotel not to have to walk to the pavement. It was not just the cabs that had to meet rigorous standards, so did those who wanted to drive them. They had to pass the dreaded 'knowledge'. For those operating in central London today that means memorising 320 standard routes and knowing 25,000 streets within a six-mile radius of Charing Cross. This can literally take years of travelling the routes, originally by bicycle but now on motor scooters, before being allowed to drive and ply for hire. In the 1960s, a new taxi service appeared in London, the minicabs. They are not allowed to pick up passengers in the street, but they were not subject to the same rules as the black cabs. Very importantly, the drivers did not and do not have to do The Knowledge. Not surprisingly, the black cab drivers were furious at what they regarded as unfair competition. I have some sympathy with them having once ordered a minicab only to find that the driver hadn't a clue where to go. I finished up directing him myself and only just arrived at the destination in time to stand as best man at my friend's wedding.

   The obvious candidate for change in public transport was the omnibus. The first motorised omnibus, powered by a Daimler engine, took to the streets for a trial run in 1898, between Kensington Gate and Victoria. It was not a success, mainly because it was fitted with metal wheels that played havoc with road surfaces. The London General Omnibus Company was quick to

A London taxi of 1908 manufactured by the French company Unic. It is now in the National Motor Museum at Beaulieu.

see that change was inevitable, and in 1905 they obtained their first motor buses. Fifty were ordered from the London company Sidney, Straker & Squire, who had started in business manufacturing steam vehicles but had turned to motors, and fifty-four were supplied by the French company De Dion-Bouton, who at the time were the largest manufacturers of automobiles in the world, turning out 2,000 cars a year. The name omnibus soon dropped out of use and the new vehicles became simply buses, and they acquired some of the features that still exist on London buses today. The Metropolitan Police insisted that as part of their licence they should display a destination board at the front with a route number, and the company decided to paint all their buses red.

In 1908, the LGOC merged with their two main rivals, the London Motor Omnibus Company and the London Road Car Co., and decided to design and build their own buses at a factory in Walthamstow. The new bus, the X-type, was very similar to the old horse omnibuses, a double-decker with an open top deck. Around 60 of these vehicles were built. The X-type was replaced by the B-type, destined to be the first reliable, mass-produced bus. They first entered service in 1911 and by 1913 there were around 2,500 in service. It was rated with a top speed of a modest 15mph which was quite adequate as the legal speed limit was only 12mph. It is a mark of how ill prepared London was for this new form of transport that none of the buses were fitted with headlamps until 1913. A working replica of a B-type operates at the Beamish open-air museum, giving modern passengers the pleasure, if that is the right word, of riding on the hard wooden seats of the top deck.

When war broke out in 1914, B-types were sent to France for troop movements. At first, they were in their gaudy colours of London days, which made them all too obvious targets, and they were soon painted khaki. The glass windows went and were replaced by planks. Altogether, around 900 buses were used on the Western Front and when the war ended, they were used to bring the troops home. With thousands of LGOC men away at the war, many jobs had to be taken by women – often very much in the public eye as bus conductresses. Once the war was over, however, they lost their jobs to the returning men. There was a shortage of buses, and lorries were pressed into temporary service, with planks as seats, until the factories could convert back from war work. Things on the roads were somewhat chaotic as there were still no fixed rules for the new generation of motorists. The Highway Code only came in

1934 and I still have a copy of my father's old AA guide from the early thirties, which simply advises drivers to move towards the left if they see another vehicle approaching.

Things were beginning to change. In 1933, the London Passenger Transport Board was formed and took over the whole fleet of some 6,000 London buses. A new generation of buses, the STL class, was designed with a covered upper deck, upholstered seats and an enclosed cab for the driver. The steady advance in bus performance and comfort came to a halt with the declaration of war in 1939. The buses continued to operate, but in nightmare conditions once the raids on London began. It was not so much the danger of being hit by a bomb, but drivers had the difficult and dangerous task of negotiating the streets, pock-marked with craters and covered in rubble. This was especially dangerous at night, when the buses had dimmed headlights.

After the war, Britain was left exhausted both physically and financially and there were shortages of basic raw materials.

The X-type
London bus. Over 1,000 of these vehicles were built between 1919 and 1926: this one dates from 1920 and was withdrawn from service in 1932.

Throughout the forties, new buses were being built in improved design, culminating in the bus that was to dominate the London scene for half a century – the Routemaster, first introduced in 1954. One feature of the new buses was the entrance right beside the driver's cab. By 1956, the first experiments were made in one-man operation, with the driver taking the fares from passengers as they entered. The pattern was set for the future development of London's buses up to the end of the twentieth century.

Today, transport in London has to face two intimately connected challenges, overcoming air

One of the many women who were employed as bus conductors during the First World War.

The L-type bus that largely replaced the X-type when it first came into use in 1929. During the Second World War, they had anti-blast curtains on the windows and shaded headlamps.

MOTOR VEHICLES • **153**

The RT bus, together with the Routemaster, dominated the London road transport scene throughout the second half of the twentieth century.

pollution and ending the emission of greenhouse gases that are triggering climate change. There were many changes made at the start of the twenty-first century, including the introduction of the so-called 'bendy buses' – articulated single deck vehicles. The idea was sound, and buses like these were common in European cities, but in practice they often had trouble negotiating the tight corners and narrow roads of London. However, when Boris Johnson was elected Mayor in 2008, he promised to get rid of them altogether and replace them with a new generation of Routemasters. It seemed to many to be more a nod to nostalgia for the old red double deckers than a practical solution for transport that fitted the needs of the day. When Sadiq Khan took over as Mayor he cancelled orders for the Routemasters after just half of the 2,000 planned had been delivered. The emphasis now would be on low emission vehicles. These included hybrid buses, using a mixture of diesel engine and electric battery-powered motor. The batteries are kept charged by using the energy generated when braking. Purely electric buses have also been introduced and a few buses that use hydrogen as a fuel. Today, the vast majority of London buses are hybrids. It is not just buses that have had to adapt to changed circumstances: in future all new taxis have to be electric and the first electric cabs have already appeared in the capital. The problem of air pollution by private cars, however, has not yet been resolved.

A hydrogen powered bus is one solution to the problem of air pollution in the capital. The gas tanks are on the top of the bus.

CHAPTER NINE

Aviation

The idea that human beings might one day be able to fly has existed since ancient times, in fables such as that of Icarus who managed to take off but got too near the sun and fell to his death. Real attempts also go back a long way. The honour, if that is the right word, of being the first Englishman to fly goes to a monk of Malmesbury Abbey, who made himself a pair of wings and leapt off a high tower in 1010. He managed to glide for about 200 yards before crashing and breaking both his legs. Attempts to emulate the birds with their flapping wings could never succeed. The first successful attempts to fly were in hot air balloons, pioneered by the Montgolfier brothers, who, in 1783, sent up the first experimental version, though the passengers for the first flight were not humans but were a sheep, a duck and a cock. Human flights followed soon after and balloon mania hit Britain, and many adventurous flights were made, not always successfully, and too many early aeronauts died while being over ambitious. London saw its first balloon flight, when the Italian Vincenzo Lunardi took off in a hydrogen balloon from the Royal Artillery Company's training ground at Moorfields in the City. He apparently thoroughly enjoyed his flight, seeing off a bottle of wine, before landing in fields near Ware in Hertfordshire.

There were to be many more balloon flights over the years, but neither the hot air balloon nor the hydrogen balloon were practical forms of transport for a very good reason; they could not be steered. The balloon went where the wind took it. I discovered the disadvantage of this myself on a flight from Goring on the Thames, when we found ourselves drifting straight for the American Air Force missile site at Greenham Common. It seemed politic to make an early landing. Steering was only really practical if the balloon also had a power source that made it independent of the wind. One of the first to propose this was Sir George Cayley in a three-part paper on aerial navigation which was published in 1809-10. What he proposed was in effect not a balloon but an airship with a light wooden frame, controlled by a rudder. This was all very sensible, but for propulsion he recommended flapping wings powered by a steam engine. He claimed that an airship

Vincenzo Lunardi in the first balloon flight from London in 1784. He is shown having just taken off from the Royal Artillery parade ground.

144 yards long could carry 50 men on a 960-mile flight. Fortunately for his reputation, it was never built. Practical airships really only came into use with the invention of the petrol engine.

Cayley, however, did have other ideas on flight and began experimenting with heavier than air machines. In the same set of papers, he described the idea of a fixed wing aircraft. He recognized that no suitable engine was available to power it, but he wrote that it would be possible to make a glider in which a man could fly. He continued to write about the subject of aeronautics, but it was not until 1849 that he built his first practical glider in which a boy 'floated off the ground for several yards'. Then in 1853, he built a larger version that was successfully flown, apparently with his coachman as pilot. The glider has not survived but he left detailed notes on how it was built, and they were used to make a replica that was successfully flown in 1972. Had the petrol engine been available, Cayley could well have beaten the Wright brothers in producing the first airplane. He had already decided that propulsion would be through a screw propeller and for stability, the plane would need a vertical tail.

Following the Wright brothers' first flight in 1903, the early years of the twentieth century saw many experiments with planes in America and Europe. The important centre in Britain in the early years was Brooklands, the car racing circuit that had been created just outside Weybridge. A.V. Roe came to the site in 1907 to build a plane, which he taxied in 1907 and towed into the air the following year. Then, in 1909, the centre of the racing circuit was cleared to create the country's first aerodrome and that October the Frenchman Louis Paulhan gave the first demonstration of powered flight to a crowd of thousands in his Farman biplane, built in France. It marked the start of Brooklands' important role in the development of flying in Britain. A flying school was established there, and among the young men who came to learn was Tommy Sopwith, who was to go on to become a major figure in aeroplane development. The Sopwith Camel was Britain's most successful fighter plane in the First World War. But for the time

Louis Paulhan in his Farman biplane with Mrs Frances Dick as a passenger in 1910.

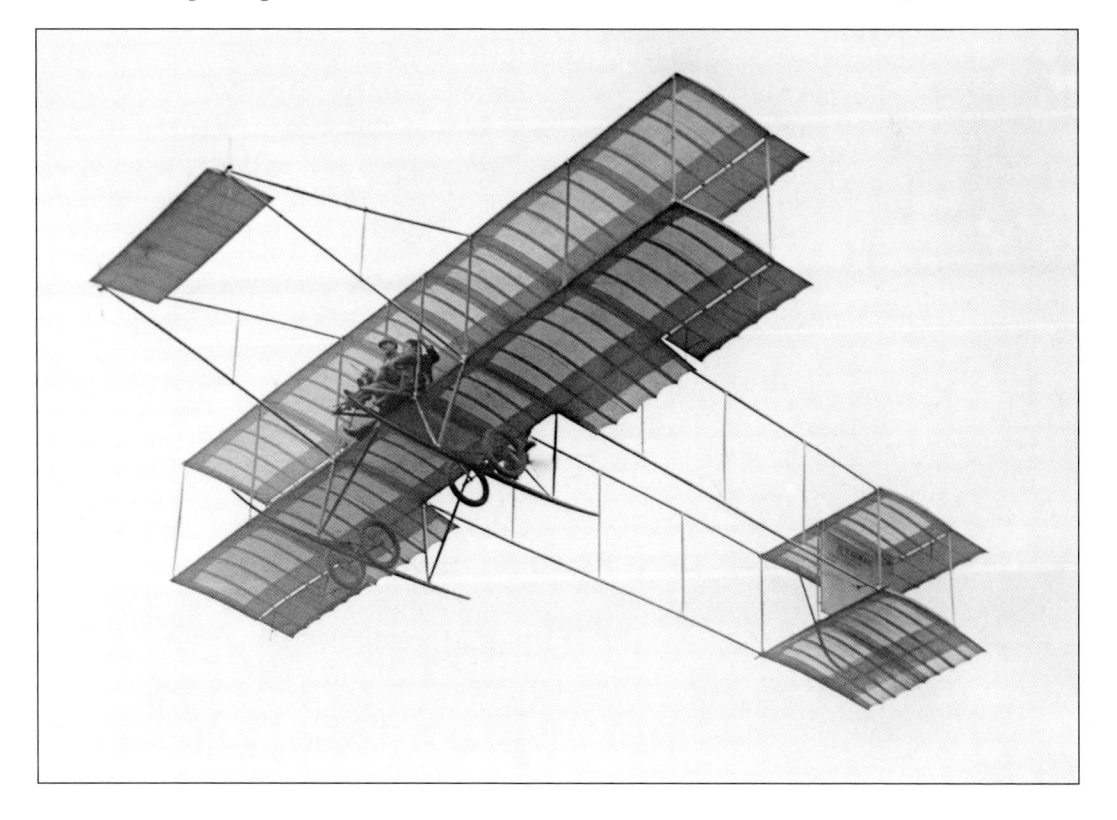

being, flying was strictly limited to rather flimsy craft piloted by adventurous young men. There was no real thought yet of passenger services, though Paulhan did give rides when he took his plane to America.

The outbreak of war in 1914 brought private flying to an end, but during the war huge advances were made in aircraft design, particularly with the large bombers that could carry heavy payloads. These were the planes that would be adapted for civilian use. The first international passenger service was run by Air Transport and Travel. They went into operation from Hounslow Heath to the west of London, close to the site of the present Heathrow Airport, in August 1919, with a single-engined De Havilland DH4A, adapted from the DH4 bomber. It flew to Le Bourget, 7 km from Paris, with just one passenger, some leather, several braces of grouse and jars of Devon cream. It has not actually been recorded, but it does suggest a celebration feast was being planned when the plane landed.

The next commercial flight followed just a week later. Handley Page Transport used one of that company's adapted twin engine bombers to fly from their base at Cricklewood in North London, also to Le Bourget. The pilot on the first flight was Lt. Col. W. Sholto Douglas who was to go on to become chairman of British Overseas Airways.

A third airline, Instone, started up in February 1920, flying out of Hounslow. It was the last to fly from that area for many years, as a brand-new airport was being developed at Croydon with far better facilities. The airport had its origins in two adjoining airfields, developed during the war years, Beddington and Waddon. It was

The De Havilland DH4 bomber was first developed during the First World War and was later developed into Britain's first passenger airliner. This plane is preserved in America.

An Air Transport and Travel DH16 passenger plane photographed c.1920.

the world's first airport to have a control tower, though it was a very basic structure – no more than a tall wooden hut with windows on all four sides. It was able to pass on useful information to the pilots by radio. Initially it was very far from what we would today consider an adequate airport and safety was distinctly basic. The old airfields had stood on either side of Plough Lane and the road was still open, so whenever a plane was about to take off, a man with a red flag had to go out and wave down any road traffic. In spite of all this, it was now London's main commercial airport, serving Paris, Rotterdam and Amsterdam.

In 1924, Handley Page and Instone were combined with two other airlines to form Imperial Airways. The new company was expected to spread its routes to different parts of the Empire, hence its name, but it started more modestly with an extension from Amsterdam to Copenhagen. In 1925, there was the first flight to Egypt, but far more impressive was the start of a service to Cape Town. The first trial run was made by Alan Cobham for the RAF, in November of that year, but it involved a whole string of stops along the way for refuelling. Even before reaching Africa, there were calls at London, Paris, Marseilles, Pisa, Taranto, and Athens and a further 21 stops before finally reaching Cape Town. On 27 December 1926 there was another ambitious flight, this time to India. The plane chosen was the DH66, named the Hercules following a competition in the Meccano Magazine. It was a three-engined biplane and where earlier planes had plywood bodies, this was steel, but with a wooden compartment suspended inside it that held the baggage, seven passengers and a radio operator. The pilot and co-pilot had to make do with an open cockpit in the nose. Given that the cruising speed was only 110mph, it is not too surprising that the flight time from Croydon to Delhi was 62 hours 27 minutes, finally arriving on 8 January.

With Imperial Airways opening up more and more routes joining London's airport to the world, it became necessary to expand Croydon and improve the facilities. Between 1926 and 1928, new hangars, a passenger terminal, a new control tower and the world's first airport hotel were built. The style for the main buildings was very much of the period, with the clean-cut lines that characterise Art Deco, but the hotel had a rather homely appearance, unlike the multi-storey, anonymous airport hotels of today.

The early aircraft had only the most basic facilities, but in 1927, the Silver Wing service was started between London and Paris, with comfortable seats and a new member of the flight crew – a steward who served a four-course lunch. The flight time was two and a half hours, which is more or less the same as the time now taken for the journey by Eurostar. It was, of course, very expensive and, later that year, a second-class service was introduced with no cabin staff and a slower journey time. For those who just wanted to sample this exciting new form of travel, there was a Silver Wing flight over London with afternoon teas for two guineas – roughly £150 today.

In 1931, Imperial Airways took delivery of a new, luxury

The passenger buildings and control tower at Croydon Airport.

aircraft from Handley Page, the HP 42. This was a large biplane with four engines that originally took just six passengers forward of the wings and twelve aft in cabins designed to emulate the luxury of the famous Orient Express. It offered exceptional comfort and full meal service but not a very quick journey, as the cruising speed was a very modest 100mph. But for its time it represented a winning combination of comfort and safety. There were some significant changes in aircraft design in the 1930s. At the opposite end of the scale from the HP42 was the Avro 652, which was a light monoplane and the first commercial airliner to have a retractable undercarriage. It was a design that lasted for many years, reappearing under a new name as the Avro Anson, when it was taken over by the RAF. I had the pleasure of briefly being allowed to take the controls of one of these planes and found it surprisingly simple to keep to a steady fight path.

Croydon continued to be London's airport that served the world, and the ultimate in long distance flights was inaugurated in 1935 with a regular service to Australia. The weekly trip to Brisbane took 12½ days – long haul flights really were long in those days. The cost for a single fare was £195, which would be a staggering £14,000 today. But this was to be the last year in which Imperial held a virtual monopoly on European flights and when all would be leaving from Croydon.

In 1930, the Surrey Aero Club had an airfield used by flying enthusiasts, but in 1934 it was given a licence to operate as a public aerodrome and was used by the small company Hillman's Airways. The idea was that it would act as a relief aerodrome when Croydon was exceptionally busy. But development was rapid, and what had been a small flying club was to become Gatwick Airport. A special railway station was opened in 1935 from which a subway led into the new smart circular departure building known as the Beehive. Its importance grew when Hillman's joined with another small company – Spartan Airlines – to create British Airways. That relationship, however, was short lived. In 1937, British Airways moved to Croydon. The owners of Gatwick, however, had the last laugh. Croydon has long since closed and Gatwick is now the country's second largest airport and just half an hour from central London by train on the Gatwick Express.

In 1938, air traffic was split between Imperial, concentrating on servicing the Empire, and British Airways, concentrating on Europe. As part of the new arrangements, BA moved yet again, this time to a place whose name hardly anyone knows these

An Imperial Airways Handley Page HP42 being refuelled on a flight to the Far East in the 1930s.

days, Heston, to the west of London. It was here that Neville Chamberlain landed in September 1938, brandishing his famous piece of paper and proclaiming, 'Peace in our time'. Then, having sliced up the overseas cake, the government decided to unite it again by combining BA and Imperial to create British Overseas Airways Corporation, BOAC. The new company had scarcely had time to organize anything before war was declared on 3 September 1939 and all civil flights were halted. The Thirties had been a time of rapid development and London had seen airports grow and prosper. But planes were still slow, comparatively small and travelling by air was very much something for the rich. The post-war years were to see big changes.

The story of the next major development of the post-war years actually begins in the 1930s, when aero engineer Richard Fairey

The original 'Beehive' passenger terminal at Gatwick airport.

bought land in Harmondsworth to create a private airfield. In the war, it was taken over by the RAF who also acquired a large stretch of former farmland next to the Fairey field and near the village of Heath Row. At the end of the war, the RAF no longer needed the airfield, and it was handed over to the Air Ministry for development into what would be London's main airport. At first, Heathrow was primitive, with no proper passenger buildings, just a set of old military marquees, with no heating. To reach the planes, passengers had to walk over wooden duckboards to keep them clear of the muddy ground. In May 1946, the new London airport was officially opened. As a further indication that a new era in air travel was opening, on 1 July a Lockheed Constellation took off for New York, though this involved stops at Shannon and Gander, Newfoundland. Planes too were changing, with a new generation that had pressurized cabins, allowing them to fly well above 10,000 ft, a height at which the lack of oxygen in the air can begin to cause problems.

Later that year, British European Airways (BEA) was formed and began their operations from Northolt. They continued to use unpressurised aircraft, including the Douglas DC3, the most successful aircraft ever built – there are still DC3s flying today over eighty years after the first plane took off from a runway. Other new designs were making such planes obsolete. Engines had been using the same technology as that which was driving all kinds of vehicles, with pistons moving up and down in a cylinder. The new generation were turbo-props, in which the hot gases from

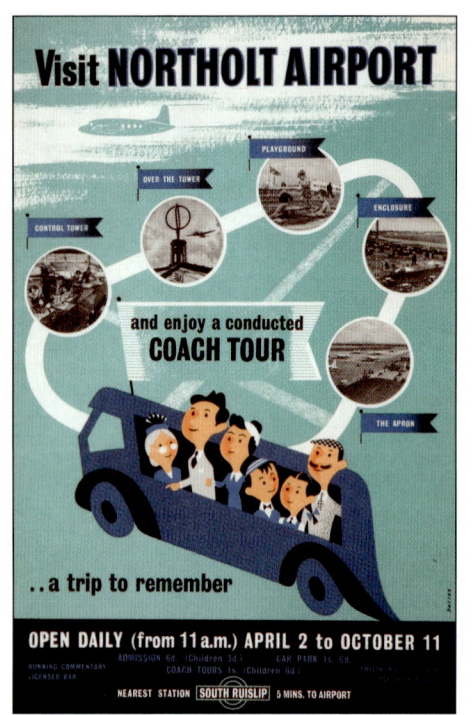

In the immediate post-war years, few could afford to fly, so a trip to the airport was the next best thing.

combustion drove the turbine. The first aircraft of this type to take off on a BEA flight from Northolt for Le Bourget in 1950 was a Vickers Viscount. But already a new type of propulsion was being developed.

Jet propulsion had been introduced into both British and German fighter planes during the war, but it was the British company De Havilland that designed the first jet airliner, the Comet. The first prototype was developed in 1949 and after extensive testing went into service with BOAC in 1952. It was an immediate success, but soon afterwards there was a worrying series of accidents, the first two of which occurred when the planes failed to take off. The first simply went off the runway with minor casualties, but the second ended in a ditch and the five crew and six passengers were killed. The accidents were put down to pilot error. In May 1953, a Comet was caught in a thunderstorm over India and crashed, killing all 43 on board. This was not pilot error and there were suspicions that there was perhaps some fundamental flaw in the aircraft. The planes, however, continued to fly, but on 10 January 1954, a BOAC plane took off from Rome and twenty minutes later broke up in mid-air, crashing into the Mediterranean. There was a committee of enquiry, but it was decided that there were no signs of any physical structural problems with the plane. But just four months later, on 8 April, another Comet crashed into

The De Havilland Comet was the world's first jet airliner. After a series of fatal accidents, it was withdrawn and redesigned. This is the later model with the rounded windows.

the Mediterranean with the loss of all on board. It was one accident too many and the entire fleet was grounded. A new investigation revealed a previously unknown phenomenon, metal fatigue. The hulls had failed due to stresses that were particularly strong round the square windows. It turned out that these windows that had been so enjoyed for the good views they gave to passengers were the main cause of the crashes, which is why all modern jets have smaller, oval windows. The remaining Comets were all withdrawn from service, and a new generation of redesigned Comets were brought back into service.

The accidents gave other aero companies time to catch up on the British manufacturer, and over the next few years the market would be dominated by the Americans, especially Boeing. But the Comets had brought in a new age of aviation. Flying that had once been reserved for the very rich became much more widely available and the introduction of cheap package holidays meant that Londoners who might once have gone to Southend or Brighton were as likely to end up on a beach in Spain. Northolt stopped operations and Heathrow steadily grew in size and importance. The old tents soon gave way to permanent structures, including the impressive 122-foot high control tower and passenger terminals. By the time Terminal 1 had opened in 1969, five million passengers a year were passing through the airport, and it would continue to grow until passenger numbers had reached 67 million with flights to 180 destinations in almost 100 different countries. Gatwick too has grown over the years and air transport has become a vital part of the life of the capital.

A postcard of Heathrow airport in the early 1970s.

CHAPTER TEN

Recent Developments

One of the biggest changes in transport for London was the development of motorways heading away from the capital to all points of the compass. There was one form of travel, however, that remained stubbornly difficult – getting round the centre. The North Circular Road was, at least, dual carriageway, but even so was a nightmare at rush hour, while the South Circular was simply a bad joke. The opening of the M25 orbital motorway was a big improvement in taking traffic round the city, though it too can notoriously get frustratingly blocked with traffic. Construction, however, presented one problem – in the east it would have to cross the wide Thames estuary. The place to do so was obvious. It would have to be Dartford, where a road tunnel already existed.

The idea for a tunnel first appeared in 1924 but work only started on a pilot tunnel in 1936 and was completed two years later. It was a success but any ideas of going ahead with the actual tunnel were abandoned at the start of the war. The austerity years after the war held back major engineering projects, but work resumed in 1959 and by 1963 it was opened as a two-lane route for which tolls were paid. When it was built, the authorities considered that it would be perfectly adequate for the expected traffic of two million vehicles a year, but within half a dozen years that had shot up to around eight million. So, a second tunnel was built to the east of the first and opened in 1976, so that each tunnel could carry one-way traffic.

Even two tunnels eventually proved inadequate for the increased traffic. There had never been a bridge across the Thames downstream from the Pool of London and one can understand why given the width of the estuary at this point. Now, however, as traffic continued to grow relentlessly, the need for a new bridge became increasingly urgent. The bridge design was by the German engineer Hellmut Homberg and consisted of two approach viaducts – 1,052 metres on the Essex side, 1,008 metres in Kent – and a central cable-stayed span of 450 metres, rising 65 metres above the river. The central deck was suspended from towers, based on immense caissons, manufactured in the Netherlands. It was a truly international operation. The bridge

Boring machine used in the construction of the first Dartford tunnel in the 1930s.

was opened by the Queen in October 1991 and named after her. With a total length of a mile and three quarters, it is an imposing structure. Everyone presumed that the traffic problems had now been solved, but as seems always to be the case, the optimism proved unfounded, and there is talk of needing yet another bridge across the lower Thames to ease the congestion.

The gap between conception of the Dartford tunnels and completion spanned half a century, but that is nothing compared

The Queen Elizabeth II bridge across the Thames at Dartford.

with the length of time that passed with the other major tunnelling programme of the time. The first proposal for a tunnel under the English Channel was made by a French engineer Albert Mathieu-Favier in 1802, who proposed a two-bore tunnel for coaches. There were to be ventilation shafts poking up from the tunnel above sea level, and a central island at which horses could be changed. Nothing came of that idea, nor was a new proposal of 1839 by another Frenchman, Aimé Thomé de Gamond, though he did carry out a geological and hydrological survey of the area between Dover and Calais. The idea popped up again in 1865 and 1866. It was only in 1876 that the French and British governments agreed that a railway tunnel would be a good thing, and the Anglo-French Submarine Railway Company was formed in 1881 and work began on pilot tunnels on both sides of the Channel. The exploratory tunnel on the English side was bored into Shakespeare Cliff, but it had only advanced about a mile when the whole project was cancelled, mainly from British insularity. There were dire warnings in the popular press that if the tunnel was completed, hordes of French soldiers would rush through and invade the country.

An early suggestion for a tunnel under the English Channel, complete with tall ventilation shaft.

There were to be more attempts to revise the idea in the early years of the twentieth century, but none came to fruition. Real progress was made in the 1960s, when the British and French governments agreed on a tunnel, with two bores to carry rail car shuttles, with a service tunnel in between. Boring machines were set underground, but once again the British pulled out, this time from a mixture of rising costs and doubts about the new European Economic Community. In 1979, the whole idea was confused by a set of different alternatives to the original rail tunnel with a car shuttle – a suspension bridge, with a series of spans – an idea that had already been advanced at the end of the nineteenth century; a tunnel between artificial islands; and a wide road tunnel. Finally, agreement was reached on the 1960s rail version and an agreement was signed in 1986 between the two governments and contracts awarded. The Channel Tunnel Group was combined with France-Manche, and it was agreed work would start from both ends and meet in the middle, which would be a new international frontier.

In all, eleven tunnel boring machines were used and work started in 1988. On 1 December 1990, the two ends met and a British worker and his French counterpart shook hands through the first opening. One of the most remarkable facts and a tribute to the engineers involved is that the two tunnels were out of alignment by only 36cm.

In 1994, the Channel Tunnel was officially opened, with the shuttle carrying trucks and cars and with passenger trains. The service originally ran from Waterloo International, using existing track. This created an immediate problem. In France, the route was using the latest electric TGV trains – the initials stand for trés grande vitesse, very great speed, and they earned the name. The trains from Paris to the tunnel had an average speed of 300 km/hour, while in England the maximum speed was just 160 km/hour. And as the same track was used by local trains, the service was limited and delays were common. It was all a bit embarrassing for the British, who had invented railways in the first place and were now looking rather pathetic. It was decided that it was essential to build a new high-speed line and provide a new generation of Eurostar electric trains to run on it. The result was known as HS1 – high speed one – and had its international terminus at St. Pancras station. As a result, a new British speed record was set at 208mph (335 km/hour) and the fastest journey time was recorded on a run from Paris to London of just over 2 hours 3 minutes. For Londoners wanting to go to France it was ideal, being able to use a station in the centre of London to reach a whole variety of different destinations in Europe. Those wanting to use their own cars have only to drive down the M20 to Folkestone to join the Shuttle. There is a neat circularity about the arrangements. When the first passenger services began on the Liverpool & Manchester Railway, passengers could sit in their own carriages on the train. Now, car owners could do the same. It may have taken 100 years since the idea of a channel tunnel was first mooted to it being accomplished, but it has been a huge success. It has also set out to show that it could keep environmental damage to a minimum. In 2007, Eurostar became the world's first carbon-neutral rail service and in 2019 it removed all single use plastics from the London-Paris service.

One of the most important changes to the life of London was the closure of the docks. They were victims of a transport revolution, in which the old system of cargo stowed in open holds gave way to containerization. The old docks could no longer cope and the business shifted downstream to the new container port at Tilbury. This left a whole area of East London in need of major redevelopment, which would certainly require an appropriate transport system. In the past, the docks had been served by the London & Blackwall Railway, but that had closed in 1966 as the traffic dwindled. The line, however, remained intact. Various

The High Speed 1 Eurostar train, developed to match the TGV on the French side of the Channel Tunnel.

proposals were put forward in the 1970s, including a plan to extend the Jubilee Line to Greenwich, which was vetoed by the government as too expensive. The situation changed, however, in 1981, with the appointment of the London Docklands Development Corporation, which had ambitious plans to create a new business and financial centre on the Isle of Dogs. London Transport began an investigation of possible new transport routes.

The first decision taken was that any new route should be overground and not part of the existing tube network. Various options were considered, but eventually it was decided that it would run from the old high level Minories station on the London & Blackwall, that would be renamed Tower Gateway, to a new station on the tip of the Isle of Dogs, to become Island Gardens. Much of the old London & Blackwall was used, but new viaduct sections had to be added, notably a viaduct right across the middle of the old West India Dock. Construction began in 1985 and the new system was opened by the Queen in 1987 as the Docklands Light Railway.

There was not much traffic at first, but that soon changed with the huge office development of Canary Wharf. What had once been little more than a modest stopping point was redeveloped as

A driverless train on the Docklands Light Railway, a key component in the development of the former London Docks area.

a major new station with three tracks and six platforms as Canary Wharf's main station. More development in the area saw the whole system develop, with an extension to the City and the Royal Docks in the early 1990s, to Greenwich and Lewisham in the late 1990s and then on to Greenwich by 2009. The increased traffic required larger trains and strengthening of parts of the infrastructure. With the staging of the 2012 Olympics at a new stadium, there was further development, culminating in an extension to Stratford International station in 2011.

What was really new about the system was that the trains did not have a driver but were fully controlled by computer. Travelling on the system for the first time it was certainly novel to be able to look straight out through the front window and not see anyone in control. There was one official on each train, named rather grandly as the Passenger Service Agent. The job entailed controlling the opening and closing of doors, providing passenger information and, rather importantly, taking control if anything went wrong. From a modest start, the DLR has become a major transport route, with 400,000 journeys every weekday. At the time of writing, plans are already in hand to replace two thirds of the present rolling stock to increase the capacity of the system.

The DLR was not the only new transport innovation to serve the developing dockland. In 1981, Brymon Airways suggested that it would be possible to establish a short take-off and landing airport in the area. To prove that the project was feasible, a Brymon pilot, Harry Gee, landed a De Havilland turboprop on Heron Quay in 1982. The new City Airport was officially opened in 1987, with a single runway just 1,080 metres long – the world's longest runway is over 5,000 metres. In its first full year of operation, it carried over 100,000 passengers, but could have carried more had it been able to take larger planes. In 1992, the runway was extended to meet the increased demand. Flying into City airport is a very different experience from the arrival at most international airports. I took a flight in a turboprop from Antwerp and the approach was quite low and decidedly interesting. We flew straight down the Thames, over Tower Bridge, turned around at Westminster and then seemed to almost nosedive down towards the landing strip. In fact, the descent is only at an angle of 5.5° but compared with the usual angle for major airports of just 3° it can seem decidedly steep. Before the Covid pandemic hit transport, the airport was handling over five million passengers a year.

To celebrate the millennium, it was decided to provide Londoners with a new footbridge from the South Bank to the City close to

The runway of City Airport stretching down the centre of the dock with the Thames tidal barrier seen to the right.

St. Paul's Cathedral. There was a competition and the winning design, known as a 'blade of light', was a steel suspension bridge, which was unusual in having the cables below the deck. The design was much admired and everyone was eager to try the new crossing, only to find that when crowds of people got on it, the whole structure swayed alarmingly. The 'blade of light' gave way to the less romantic 'wobbly bridge'. It was closed two days after its opening on 10 June 2000 and was reopened in 2002 after strengthening; happily, it wobbled no more. There was a bonus for anyone with physical handicaps who wanted to cross the bridge and visit St. Paul's – a short funicular railway was set up beside the steps leading from the river to the cathedral.

The twenty-first century also saw the completion of one other new river crossing, a cable car service from Greenwich to the Royal Victoria Dock. Opened in 2012, the cables carry thirty-four gondolas at a time, each able to hold ten passengers. It is seen as more of a tourist attraction than a practical transport route, and consequently the cars move quite slowly, making the crossing in ten minutes, so that passengers can enjoy the view. In busy times, if used by commuters, journey times are halved. The system was designed to carry up to 250,000 passengers a week, but has never got anywhere near that figure. There was a flurry of interest when it first opened, but then numbers dropped off to around 10 per cent of maximum capacity. It has not, so far, been a great success.

The future of transport in the capital is uncertain. There are two factors which are going to be vital in deciding what happens next. The first is particular to the city – air pollution. The other

The Millennium bridge leading towards St. Paul's Cathedral. When first opened it swayed alarmingly, earning it the name 'wobbly bridge' – it no longer wobbles.

affects everyone – global warming. They are connected. Much of the pollution is due to vehicle exhausts, from petrol and, more damagingly, diesel vehicles, and the exhaust gases also add to the greenhouse effect. The move to greener vehicles has already begun, with electric and hydrogen power coming in for both buses and taxis. It can only be a matter of time before petrol and diesel vehicles become as rare as horses and carriages. When the first electric taxi appeared in London in 1898, it enjoyed a short period of success. Now the electric cabs are back, but rather more efficient. Electrification of the rail system has been moving steadily onwards. One area where progress is slow is air travel. There has been pressure for a third runway at Heathrow for years, which has been opposed by environmentalists of all political parties. But technology does not stand still. It is not beyond reason that new forms of plane will be developed that do not rely on fossil fuels for power.

One thing is certain: traffic in London will change just as it has always changed over the centuries.

A new tourist attraction: the cable car with the O2 arena in the background.

Further Reading

Betjeman, John, *London's Historic Railway Stations*, 1972
Bird, Anthony, *Roads and Vehicles*, 1973
Burton, Anthony, *On the Rails*, 2004
Christopher, John, *The London Bus Story*, 2007
Dyos, H.J. and Aldcroft, D.H., *British Transport*, 1969
Halford-MacLeod, Guy, *Britain's Airlines (3 vols.)*, 2006-10
Joyce, J., *London's Trams*, 1990
Singer, Charles et al (ed), *A History of Technology (7 vols.)*, 1954-78
Woodley, Charles, *History of British European Airways*, 2016

Acknowledgements

The author wishes to think the following for supplying illustrations that appear on the pages indicated in the following list.

Acabashi, 153 Alan Sorrel, 11; Alex Muller, 57 (bottom); Arpingstone, 121; Ben Brooksbrank, 136; Bernard Gagron, 9; Buckinghamshire Railway Centre, 99; California Historic Society Collection, 157; Carlisle Museum, 10; Chris Simpson, 124 (bottom); Colin 93 (bottom); David Gubler, 171; Delacto, 145; Elisha Whittesley Fund, 47; Ffestiniog Railway, 101, 102; George Rex,86; Gill Scott, 32, 33; Hammersfan, 122; Islington Libraries, 129; Jason Peper,30; J.S. Bond, 158; Justinc, 39; Kate Onan, 53; Library of Congress,56, 162; London Transport Museum, 40, 152 (bottom); Magnus D, 50; Mike McBey, 173; Motmit,71; Museum of London, 46 (top); Museum of London Dockland, 52; National Motor Museum, 149; National Postal Museum, 52; National Railway Museum, 87,88; Nobert Nagal, 8; Peter Trimming, 137;RalfManteufel, 164 (bottom); R.C. Riley Collection, 123; Rex Gray, 148; Robert Cuffs, 13; Romezar, 175; Ruthas, 103; Shadowsettle, 85; Simon Edwards, 132; Southwark Library Service, 130; Spsmiller, 154; State Library Nuremberg, 14; Tate Gallery, 51 (bottom); Tecmeister, 89, The Enegineer,106,139; Tom Brogden, 43; Tristan Surtel, 174; University of Toronto, 117 (bottom); Unsplash, 95; UPY611,168; Valentine,68 (bottom); Yale Centre for British Art, 105 (top).

Index

Adams, William, 99
Aircraft: early, 157-8; passenger planes, early, 159-63; passenger planes, jet, 164-5
Airports: Brooklands, 157; City, 173; Croydon, 158-9, 160-1; Gatwick, 161; Heathrow, 158, 163, 165; Heston, 162; Hounslow, 158; Northolt, 163, 165
Air Transport & Travel, 158
Anglo-French Submarine Railway Co., 168
Austen, Jane, 28-9

Bailey, Captain, 34
Balloons, hot air and hydrogen, 155
Barker & Co., 29, 147
Barlow, Peter, 118
Barry, John Wolfe, 67
Bazalgette, Joseph, 49, 58
Beattie, Joseph Hamilton and William, 98
Beck, Harry, 127
Becket, Thomas, 15
Bentley, W.O, 143-6
Benz, Karl, 140
Benz, Martha, 140
Bersey, Walter Charles, 138
Besant, John, 36
Betjeman, Sir John, 88, 121
Birkenhead, 129
Blackpool, 132

Blenkinsop, John, 73
Bonner, Charles, 36
Boudica, 7
Boulton & Watt, 46
Braddock, H.W., 96
Bramah, Joseph, 40
Bridges: Battersea, 49-50; Blackfriars, 7, 53-4; Clifton, 48; Hammersmith, 58; Hungerford, 58, 92; London, old, 15-17, 54; London, new, 54-5; Millennium, 173-4; Pulteny, 17; Putney, 48-9; Queen Elizabeth II, 166-7; Tower, 67-9, 118; Union, 57; Westminster, 50-3
British Airways, 161
British European Airways, 163
British Overseas Airways, 158
British Overseas Airways Corporation, 162
Brixton, 12
Bromley-on-Bow, 12
Brown, Samuel, 56
Brunel, Isambard Kingdom, 58, 63-7, 82-4
Brunel, Marc, 61-7, 118
Butler, Edward, 140

Cable car, 174
Campbell, Malcolm, 146
Canaletto, 52
Carts, Roman, 10; medieval, 16-18
Cayley, Sir George, 155-7

Channel Tunnel Group, 169
Chaucer, Geoffrey, 15
Coach types, Sociable, 27;
　Clarence, 28; Brougham, 28;
　Lord Mayor's, 29
Coaches, early, 23-4; later
　developments, 25-30; steam,
　30-34; stage and mail, 34-7; post
　chaise, 37-8; Hansom cab, 44-5
Coaches, railway: early,
　102-6; Pullman, 106-7;
　Coronation, 108
Crossing sweepers, 45
Croydon Council, 136
Cursus publicus, 10

Daimler, Gottlieb, 140
De Dion-Bouton, 150
Decker, Thomas, 12
Domesday Book, 12

Edward III, 13
Edward VII, 120
Electric telegraph, 111-12
Electromobile, 138
Elizabeth I, 23
Elliot, Obadiah, 27
Escalators, 122
Eurostar, 88
Evelyn, John, 24

Fairey, Richard, 62
Felton, William, 29, 30
Fothergille, William, 111
Fowler, John, 115-6

Gamond, Aimé Thomé de, 168
Gas engine, 139
Gas lighting, 45-7, 105
Gooch, Daniel, 98, 115
Gooch, John, 98

Gough map, 12
Grantham, John, 131
Griffith, Julius, 40

Hallidie, Andrew Smith, 131
Hancock, Walter, 41-4
Hansom, Joseph, 44-5
Hardwick, Philip, 81
Hawkins, John, 10-12
Henry II, 15
Hillman's Airways, 161
Hobson, Samuel, 29-30
Holden, Charles, 123
Homberg, Hellmut, 166
Huskisson, William, 108
Huygens, Christian, 138

Imperial Airways, 159-60
Ironbridge, 54

Jones, Sir Horace, 67

Kitchiner, Dr., 36

Laffitte, Jacque, 38
Lanchester, Frederick, 140
Leicester Square, 24
Lenoir, Etienne, 139
Locomotive constructors:
　George England, 100-1;
　Fairlie, 101; London & South
　Western Railway, 98-9; North
　London, 99;
Londinium, 7-10
London County Council, 134
London Electric Cab Co., 138
London General Omnibus Co.,
　128, 149-51
London Hydraulic Co., 118
London & Paddington Steam
　Carriage Co., 42

London Passenger Transport
    Board, 123, 135, 151
London Regional Transport, 136
London United Tramways, 131-2
London & Westminster Chartered
    Gas Light & Coal Co., 47
Lunardi, Vincenzo, 155

Malmsbury monk, 155
Mary I, 23
Mathieu-Favier, Albert, 168
McAdam, John Loudon, 22-3
Metroland, 121
Metropolitan Electric
    Tramways, 134
Montgolfier brothers, 155
Motor buses: X-type,
    150; B-type, 150-1;
    Routemaster, 152, 154; bendy,
    154; low emission, 154
Motor cars: Mercedes Benz,
    140; Butler, 140; Lanchester,
    140; James & Browne, 140-1;
    Vauxhall, 142-3, 147; Bentley,
    143-6; Rolls Royce, 146;
    Napier, 146-7
Motorcycle, 140, 143-4
Murdoch, William, 45-7
Murray, Matthew, 73
Mylne, Robert, 53

Napier, David
Newcomen, Thomas, 30-1
Nine Elms, 98
North Metropolitan Tramway
    Co., 130

Okuno, Frank, 33
Omnibus, horse drawn, 38-40;
    steam, 40-4
Otto, Nicolaus, 139

Palmer, John, 35-6
Paoletti, Roland
Paulham, Louis, 157-8
Pavage, 13
Paviers, 13-15
Pearson, Charles, 113
Pepys, Samuel, 26
Pitt, William, 35
Pompeii, 7
Pyne, William Henry, 27

Races to the North, 102
Railways: Docklands Light,
    170-3; Eastern Counties,
    103-4; Ffestiniog, 101; Great
    Central, 96; Great Eastern,
    94-6; Great Northern,
    85-6, 114-5; Great Western,
    82-4, 104, 114-5; HS1, 170;
    Killingworth, 73-4; Liverpool
    & Manchester, 74-5, 108,
    170; London & Birmingham,
    79-82, 114; London &
    Blackwall, 89, 170; London
    & Brighton, London,
    Brighton & South Coast,
    78;77, 94; London, Chatham
    & Dover, 91-2;London &
    Croydon, 77, 90-1;London
    & Greenwich, 75-8; London
    & North Eastern, 108;
    London & North Western, 94;
    London & South Western,
    70, 78; North London,
    96-7;Middleton, 73; Midland,
    87-8;Penydarren, 71-2; South
    Eastern, 77-8; Southern, 94;
    Surrey Iron, 70, 129; Victoria
    Station & Pimlico, 94;
    Volk, 119; West of London &
    Crystal Palace, 94

Railways, underground: City & South London, 118-9; Crossrail, 126; District, 116, 120; East London, 118; Jubilee line, 125-6; Metropolitan, 113-6, 120-1; Northern Line, 120, 123; Tower Subway Co., 118; Victoria line, 125
Rennie, John, 54, 59,
Roads, Roman: 7-10; medieval, 10-15; turnpike, 21-3; motorways, 166
Roe, A.V., 157
Rowland, Mike, 17

Scavengers, 13-14
Scott, John, 20-1
Scott, Sir Gilbert, 88
Sedan chair, 24-5
Shillibeer, George, 38-40, 75
Sholto Douglas, Lt. Col. W, 158
Sidney Straker & Squire, 150
Siemens, Werner Von, 119
Signalling, railway, 110-12
Sopwith, Tommy, 157
South Metropolitan Tramways & Lighting, 134
Spitalfields, 24
Stations: Cannon Street, 92; Charing Cross, 91-2; Euston, 81-2; Fenchurch Street, 89; King's Cross, 85-6, 122; London Bridge, 77; Marylebone, 95; Paddington, 83-4; St. Pancras, 87-8, 92, 170; Victoria, 94
Stephenson, George, 73-4, 110
Stephenson, Robert, 75, 80, 85, 89
Stevens, John Hargrave, 113, 114

Taxis, electric, 138, 175; motor, 147-9
Taylor, John, 23-4
Telford, Thomas, 22-3, 54, 57
Thames tunnel, Trevithick, 58-61; Brunel, 61-7; Dartford tunnel 166-7, Channel, 168-70
Thrupp, John, 29
Tower of London, 7
Train, George Francis, 128-9
Trams: horse-drawn, 128-30; steam, 130-1; cable, 131-2; electric, 132-5, 136-7
Trolley buses, 135-6;
Trésaguet, Pierre, 21-2
Trevithick, Richard, 31-4, 58-61, 71-2

Unic taxi, 148

Vaizie, Robert, 59
Vidler, John, 36
Volk, Magnus, 119

Walpole, Robert, 48
Watt, James
Wellington, Duke of, 65
Wheatstone, Charles, 111
Wheelwrights, 17-18
Whirlicotes, 19
Whistler, James, 50
William II, 15
Wilson, Alexander, 142
Winzer, Friedrich, 46-7
Wordsworth, William, 53
Wren, Christopher, 24
Wyatt, Matthew Digby, 84